FOREWORD

Carmarthenshire is an ancient county, created in 1284 ⌁⌁⌁ ⌁⌁⌁⌁
Welsh enemy Llewellyn ap Gruffydd's lands. The coun⌁⌁
royal county and lordship of Carmarthen and the lands either side of the river Tywi. This
has always been a sparsely populated, largely rural area with no great sources of wealth. As
a result, the county's historic parks and gardens were largely of modest extent and
ambition. However, there are a few notable exceptions. Head and shoulders above the
rest are the great park of Plas Dinefwr, the park and its string of lakes at Middleton Hall
(National Botanic Garden of Wales) and the seventeenth-century garden of Aberglasney.
Happily these are for the most part well preserved and cared for and are visited and
appreciated by thousands. Some parks and gardens of great historic importance, however,
such as Hywel Dda's tenth-century deer park near Whitland Abbey, speak to us only
through records and legend.

This book came into being as a result of the re-launch of the Carmarthenshire branch of
the Welsh Historic Gardens Trust. The Welsh Historic Gardens Trust aims to preserve
the rich heritage of parks and gardens across Wales. It campaigns to save them from
neglect, indifference and insensitive planning and planting. To do this the new branch
needed information. You cannot protect or preserve a park or garden if you do not know
where it is and what it contains. The most comprehensive reference available is the *Register
of Historic Parks and Gardens of Special Interest in Wales* compiled by Cadw in the late 1990s,
which includes 19 sites of national importance in Carmarthenshire. There are many more
unregistered parks and gardens and, although perhaps not of national importance, they
are still an important part of the social, cultural and historic fabric of the county. They
deserved to be rediscovered, studied and brought together in a single volume on the Parks
and Gardens of Carmarthenshire, for everyone to enjoy.

Funded by the Heritage Lottery Fund, the Welsh Church Fund, and the Carmarthenshire
Antiquarian Society, a group of volunteers set about discovering the parks and gardens in
Carmarthenshire. This included scanning old maps and newspapers, searching on line,
reading histories of the county, trips to the Royal Commission on the Ancient and
Historical Monuments of Wales and the National Library of Wales and searching their
online catalogues and databases. Volunteers visited the County Museum, the libraries in
Carmarthen and Llanelli, made trips to visit the parks and gardens that have been
included in this book, and talked to their current owners. While Dinefwr, Middleton and
Aberglasney are open to the public, many of the gardens are in private ownership and
access to them was made by invitation. Many properties have changed hands over the
years, but one or two have remained in the ownership of the same family down the

generations, and have retained a wealth of old photographs and information about their design, creation and planting.

There are a great many parks and gardens in the county worthy of research, but space and funding have dictated that a sample have been brought together in this book. Those in the Cadw register were the first to be considered for inclusion, the others were chosen as good examples of their period or type. The research will continue beyond the publication of this book and the findings, together with the archive that has already been compiled in its writing, will be uploaded onto the Historic Environment Record and will continue to be available to assist in future research.

This book could not have been written without the support of the Dyfed Archaeological Trust, who provided not only access to the Historic Environment Record, but also help and advice and a place for volunteers to meet. The contributors to the book were: Angela Adams Rice, Kate Arblaster, Joseph Atkin, Edward Davies, Brian Dix, Judith Holland, Mike Ings, Tom Lloyd, Ken Murphy, Patricia and Douglas Neil, Alice Pyper, Robert Thomas and Helen Whitear. Each section includes the name of its author. A wealth of gratitude is due to all those who helped in the research for the book, like Peter Davis and Dr J C Davies who generously provided images, and particularly to the generosity of the current owners and custodians who allowed us to visit their gardens and record them.

We hope that the information we have gathered and recorded here will enable us to promote the aims of the Welsh Historic Gardens Trust. By identifying and describing parks and gardens of historic interest we will contribute to their protection and encourage all to appreciate their value. We also hope that you enjoy delving into this rich and varied heritage of the county's historic parks and gardens of all shapes and sizes and that it inspires you both to find out more and to visit those that are open to the public. Some of the gardens included in this book are open to the public, but many are in private hands and have no public access.

Elizabeth Whittle

President

Welsh Historic Gardens Trust

CONTENTS

INTRODUCTION

Carmarthenshire Parks and Gardens within an Historical Context

Gardens and related parkland are not simply assemblages of trees and other plants arranged in neat flower beds, ornamental orchards, or some other design. They equally reflect technical and scientific advances in methods of cultivation, including plant sourcing and propagation. They are thus an indicator of past as well as present trends in horticulture and can demonstrate the adoption of the latest fashions, ideas, and taste in gardening. Yet, such places are not solely cultural artefacts. Their character and content attest the personality of individual garden-makers, subsequent owners, and other users.

Choices in design will often reflect personal concerns and feelings, together with other perceptions and thoughts. Ultimately, parks and gardens are about individuals who created and fashioned them, those who worked there, and others who visited them. They are important social documents, wherein the differences between individual sites may relate not just to size and means of wealth but can also reflect varied concepts, even at times containing encoded messages.

In taking up different ideas, individual owners might sometimes be in the vanguard of development but at other times lag behind the advances made elsewhere. The significance and meaning of gardens may therefore change just as much as their form and flora, which develop over time and can vary from one place to another.

Some Carmarthenshire parks and gardens, like Dinefwr Park on the western outskirts of Llandeilo, have been continuously created, replanted, extended, and rearranged over the course of more than four centuries. With other more recent examples presented here, they illustrate many of the wider trends in the development of Early Modern garden design. The selection of sites extends across time from the Middle Ages to the twentieth century and forms a representative sample from almost 600 historically attested gardens in the county.

Individual places range in size from large, enclosed medieval parkland and later landscaped estates, often covering many tens of acres and containing specialised areas for kitchen gardens as well as pleasure grounds, to smaller municipal or public parks, lesser household gardens, and shared allotment holdings. The scope therefore is from the high status landscapes of the county's elite to the places used for recreation, refreshment, and other relaxation by its ordinary folk. All are considered using several kinds of evidence, from various types of archival records including historic plans and views, to archaeological inquiry through the analysis of surviving physical traces. The results from remote-sensing methods such as geophysical survey techniques and air photographic analysis have also been employed, together with the identification of upstanding field remains.

The medieval period is a natural starting point for any consideration of the county's historic parks and gardens. Some form of garden, perhaps containing a sheltered orchard, might be expected around courtly residences, in addition to larger areas being created at higher status castle and monastic sites. At Laugharne Castle, for example, few physical traces have so far been identified apart from fishponds and the excavated remains of a sixteenth-century fountain. Such evidence that we possess at present largely derives from documentary sources, which mostly refer to parks like those at Abermarlais, first mentioned in 1531, and Cyffig which was created by Sir John Perrot of Laugharne Castle in Elizabethan times. Whilst the parks were primarily enclosures for storing live meat in the form of cattle and deer they would often supply various building materials, including timber which was also grown to be cut for fuel. Although not specifically designed in an aesthetic way, the individual parts of an estate and its built components might be carefully arranged to project an image of status and authority.

New ways of thinking, inspired by Renaissance ideas and growing secularity but also enabled by increasing wealth, led to a greater connection between architecture and setting. Buildings and their surroundings would now be linked in grandiose layouts that might be enhanced by terracing and other engineering work.

The features of the grandest gardens attached to the greater houses were soon adapted to smaller estates. Symmetrical gardens were laid out in a unified design based upon mathematical proportions and usually comprising a series of connected courtyards and other compartments with axially aligned gateways. Paths might run between them and join crosswalks around central features like fountains and sundials or other ornaments. A possible contemporary gatehouse and other courtyard remains can also be seen at Aberglasney, although the evidence for the Renaissance-style garden which has been reconstructed there is disputed.

The introduction of baroque ideas from France at the time of Charles II's restoration brought an emphasis on the central axis, which might additionally be marked by a formal canal and could be extended by avenues into the countryside. With the accession of William and Mary in 1688 a more intimate scale of gardening developed and there was a greater emphasis upon displaying specimen flowers as well as evergreens.

A typical late seventeenth-century geometrical arrangement of gardens is depicted in contemporary paintings of Newton House, the former seat of the Rice family in Dinefwr Park. The mid-century house is shown prior to later remodelling and is located within a series of ornamental parterres containing clipped topiary. Outside, there is a series of formal avenues from which a few trees still survive. Archaeology has demonstrated that buried remains of the gardens also exist.

The political and social upheavals of the seventeenth century combined with developments in trade, science, and technology, to usher in a period of intense creativity in garden design.

Advances in horticulture and woodland management were accompanied by piecemeal redevelopment of garden landscapes to provide greater variety, for example through contrasting areas of light and shade and the creation of sudden views and more distant vistas. The scale of working fitted well with the latest notions of extent and prospect, although the aesthetics remained largely those of the formal parks and gardens that were derived from continental models. The introduction of winding walks and other serpentine forms such as sweeping curves nevertheless denotes the adoption of a less structured approach to landscaping and the eventual loosening of the underlying geometry with its straight avenues and straight-edged canals.

The transition towards freer design was associated with a new feeling for Nature and Landscape, in which agriculture would become closely integrated with parkland planning and management. The rise of professional landscaping in the middle years of the eighteenth century is typified by the career of Lancelot 'Capability' Brown but there were other important practitioners too. Brown visited Dinefwr in 1775, where George Rice and his wife Cecil Talbot had already extended and replanted the park. He may have been responsible for the creation of the Precipice Walk and appears to have recommended re-siting the kitchen garden further away from the house. Status was now asserted by the rejection of any hint of direct or close involvement in such practical matters as fruit and vegetable growing.

Detached walled gardens are known from several other eighteenth century and later sites in the county such as at Edwinsford and Llwynywermod, (formerly known as Llwynyworwmood). Most, however, lie abandoned or are semi-derelict today. Originally they may have contained one or more heated glasshouses that could be used for growing peaches and pineapples as well as vines. In 1781, for example, John Vaughan built a new hot house at Golden Grove. Several fishponds are also recorded there, possibly to provide an opportunity for sport as well as supplying fresh fish for the table. Newly excavated lakes could be similarly stocked. As at Llwynywermod and Middleton Hall, they might be created by damming the course of a local river or stream.

Whilst the combination of 'water, wood and ground' in a beautiful form was the stock-in-trade of the professional landscaper who carefully designed such elements to appear natural, to others their scenery seemed bland, and real or true nature appeared to be lost. For them, nature was most attractive in its wild and unadorned state. The experience of crossing rough, uneven terrain was therefore to be savoured, especially if the destination was something as awesomely terrifying as the thunderous waterfall at Glynhir, for example. Equally exhilarating, though obviously much calmer, was the feeling that could be engendered when approaching Paxton's Tower (Nelson's Tower), the eye-catcher that is to be seen from the Middleton Hall Estate. The peek-a-boo views and gradually unfolding vistas are a typical picturesque device.

Romantic sentiment was eventually to be rejected in gardening during the nineteenth century. Whilst acknowledging (and encouraging) the use of a range of styles which might combine both formal and naturalistic elements, the unnatural character of most such garden design came to be fully recognised and was admired for itself.

The development of innovative and artistic arrangements accompanied a renewed interest in horticulture. Plant hunters were now searching the world to bring unusual specimens back to Britain, where improved hot houses and other technical innovations enabled them to be grown and propagated in the cooler climate. The increasingly widespread availability of new varieties and different coloured types led to the development from the mid-nineteenth century onwards of intricate and sometimes exotic bedding schemes. Artistry combined with plantsmanship in a variety of independent, imaginative, and original ways which were not wholly confined to floral schemes at larger houses nor to those in more modest private gardens. Public parks and gardens specially created as places for recreational use by nearby inhabitants often contained ornamental flower beds and occasionally an arboretum among other amenities.

The once privately owned arboretum that was established at Golden Grove in about 1860 now forms part of the country park that was created when the County Council acquired the leasehold nearly a hundred years later. The grounds of Parc Howard are likewise a public park following the gift of the property previously known as Bryn-y-Caerau to the town of Llanelli in the early twentieth century. Today, the park contains a bandstand together with children's play areas, tennis courts, and a bowling green in addition to formal gardens which feature massed flower beds. A similar mix of playground and other amenities can be found in many other parks, including Carmarthen which opened on Easter Monday 1900 and Ammanford, which, despite not being laid out until the 1930s, occupies an earlier site that had been used for sports. The previous use of Pembrey Country Park could not be more different, however, and it preserves remains associated with the explosives factories that were on the site.

Whilst the Old Bishop's Palace and part of the surrounding parkland at Abergwili are now publicly owned, much of its present character is largely due to the landscaping works of two early nineteenth-century bishops of St Davids, who introduced views and planting in keeping with contemporary taste. Fashionable bedding, specimen and exotic trees and shrubs also characterise a number of the lesser gardens that were formed from this period until the end of the century, by which time the stiffness and regimented colour schemes of the later Victorian garden was already giving way to more exuberant and informal styles of planting.

Examples of Victorian gardens include Glynhir, with its earlier picturesque walks, and Derwydd Mansion nearby. Contemporary historical maps and other sources attest the presence of other mid- to later nineteenth-century gardens at both Pantglas Hall and Tregib Mansion but, like the houses they belonged to, they have been largely destroyed. The previous loss to fire of Maesycrugiau Manor, Llanllwni, however, was followed by rebuilding accompanied by a new garden. Although since altered, this retains an unusual summerhouse designed by Messenger & Co. Ltd of Loughborough in 1906. At that time the company was one of the leading manufacturers of glasshouses in the country. In 1894 they had supplied a stove and plant-house to Derwydd Mansion and another of their installations in the county is the recently restored conservatory at Broadway, Laugharne.

A further example of an Edwardian garden survives at Llanmiloe House, near Pendine, comprising a series of terraces laid out around 1908 in grounds otherwise largely planted with woody exotics and rhododendrons. One of the finest collections of such plants in the county, however, is at Gellideg which contains many interesting and unusual trees and shrubs. Although planted only as recently as the mid-1960s onwards, it reuses earlier garden spaces and gives them an appropriate new life. This kind of 'revalorization' which recognises and revives the historical values of a site is one of several ways to conserve the rich heritage of Carmarthenshire's historic parks and gardens.

Brian Dix
Archaeologist

Opposite: Map showing parks and gardens mentioned in the text.

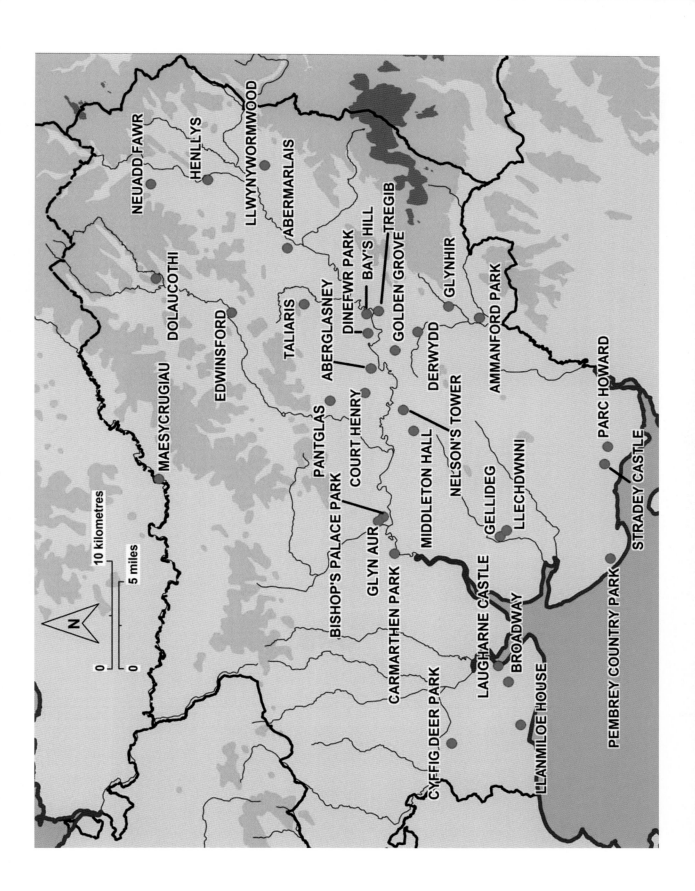

NEUADD FAWR

HENLLYS

LLWYNYWORMWOOD

ABERMARLAIS

DOLAUCOTHI

BAY'S HILL

TREGIB

DINEFWR PARK

GOLDEN GROVE

GLYNHIR

EDWINSFORD

TALIARIS

ABERGLASNEY

AMMANFORD PARK

DERWYDD

MAESYCRUGIAU

PANTGLAS

COURT HENRY

NELSON'S TOWER

PARC HOWARD

BISHOP'S PALACE PARK

MIDDLETON HALL

GELLIDEG

LLECHDWNNI

GLYN AUR

STRADEY CASTLE

CARMARTHEN PARK

LAUGHARNE CASTLE

BROADWAY

PEMBREY COUNTRY PARK

CYFFIG DEER PARK

LLANMILOE HOUSE

N

10 kilometres

5 miles

0

0

Archaeology and Gardens

K Murphy

Garden archaeology was a late addition to the discipline of archaeology, not becoming commonplace in Britain until the 1980s, although the recognition that historic gardens have an archaeological dimension goes back to the 1920s and 1930s.

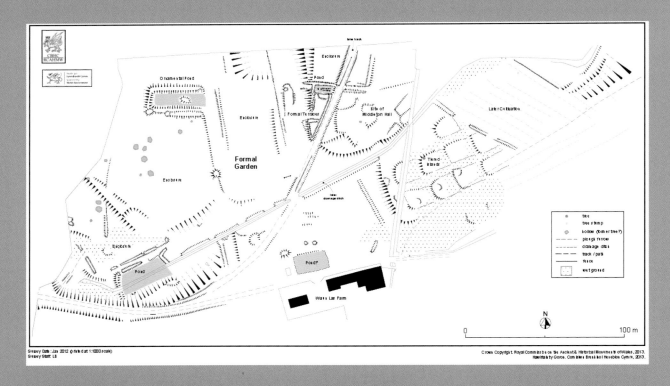

An earthwork plan of Middleton Old Hall by Louise Barker of the Royal Commission on the Ancient and Historical Monuments of Wales showing former formal gardens and water gardens.
© Crown copyright: RCAHMW

ARCHAEOLOGY AND GARDENS

Garden archaeology was a late addition to the discipline of archaeology, not becoming commonplace in Britain until the 1980s, although the recognition that historic gardens have an archaeological dimension goes back to the 1920s and 1930s. Initial studies were limited to surveying the earthworks of abandoned gardens and interpreting them using methodologies derived from studying prehistoric hill-forts or medieval castles. Now a wide range of archaeological techniques – excavation, geophysical survey, aerial photography, palaeo-environmental analysis and scientific dating – is frequently used by those studying gardens. In Wales the archaeological study of historic gardens is not as well advanced as elsewhere in the UK and there is nothing to compare with the large-scale investigations at Hampton Court, Castle Bromwich, Kenilworth Castle and Audley End, for example. However, some important work has been undertaken in Carmarthenshire, with most of the larger-scale work done to inform garden restoration, as at Aberglasney, Dinefwr Park and Middleton Hall (National Botanic Garden of Wales). This short account reviews some of the work undertaken and the techniques employed.

Richard Avent carried out the first garden archaeology in the county, rather unwittingly, during excavation in the inner ward of Laugharne Castle in 1978. Part of a circular stone fountain surrounded by a decorative cobble surface was revealed with, remarkably, a groove surviving in the soil which must have carried a lead feed-pipe for the fountain. There can be little doubt that this is the '*very proper fountaine*' described in a survey of 1595, following the death of Sir John Perrot three years earlier. Perrot was transforming the castle from medieval fortress to Tudor mansion, and part of his plan was the creation of a garden which the survey describes as '*by estimation one acre consisting of seven burgages and a half part lately built*'. The survey intimates that Perrot obtained the seven and a half burgages from burgesses of the town by underhand means. This is one of the earliest references to a garden in the county, and it would be of great interest to investigate if anything remains other than the fountain.

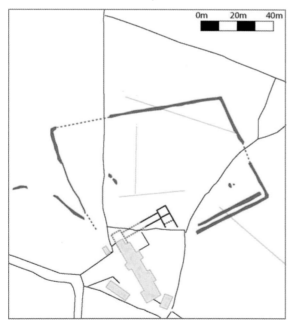

0m 20m 40m

Plan of Llys Brychan Roman villa. The foundations of the villa are marked in blue with the garden enclosure in red – evidence from excavation and geophysical survey. The present farmhouse is in yellow (drawing: Dyfed Archaeological Trust)

Archaeology has not revealed any medieval gardens in Carmarthenshire, unlike, for example, the garden excavated and restored at Haverfordwest Priory, Pembrokeshire, but it is highly likely that some castles and monasteries in Carmarthen did have gardens. Interestingly, a possible garden has been identified at Llys Brychan, the only known Roman villa in the county. The villa was excavated in the 1970s. It was not until 2009, when a geophysical survey was undertaken, that the building was found to lie within a trapezoidal enclosure, possibly a garden or orchard.

Excavation at Dinefwr Park by Dyfed Archaeological Trust (photograph: Dyfed Archaeological Trust)

Geophysical survey is a particularly valuable tool when investigating relatively large land areas and was used to great effect at Dinefwr Park. It has been suggested that the formal gardens to the north and west of the great house shown on paintings of about 1700 were aspirational, and never existed (see the Dinefwr Park entry). A geophysical survey clearly showed that the formal garden had existed, and a targeted small-scale excavation demonstrated that in the late eighteenth century, when formal gardens became unfashionable and the landscape park was created, the walls and towers of the formal garden had been dismantled and the paths and flower beds flattened. The whole was turfed over and rolling grassland taken right up to the foot of the house.

The cold bath or bathhouse in Dinefwr Park was excavated in 2007 during a programme of restoration. Bathhouses found favour with the gentry in the early- to mid-eighteenth century. Some were functional bathing places, others seem to have served as summerhouses or pavilions, but they were expensive and could be afforded only by the wealthiest landowners. The Dinefwr example lies at the outflow of a powerful spring with a plunge pool suitable for bathing. Only foundations survive of this small but elegant structure, with the plunge pool possibly lined with marble. It is interesting to note that of the three bathhouses in Carmarthenshire two have been archaeologically investigated (Dinefwr and one at Middleton Hall) and the third (also at Middleton Hall) was investigated in late 2015, but the results are not yet available. John Nash's design for a bathhouse at Golden Grove was never executed.

The work on the Middleton Hall bathhouse in the mid-1980s, during restoration carried out by the then Dyfed County Council, was the first planned excavation of a garden feature in the county. The excavation showed it to be a modest, fairly utilitarian structure, constructed of brick and timber with a plaster finish, and the plunge pool lined with blue-glazed tiles. A contemporary painting confirms the unpretentious character of the building. The above structure lies fairly close to the house: the other is in a more remote location on the estate. A contemporary painting shows a more ornate building, which perhaps functioned as a summerhouse rather than a bathing place.

The greatest amount of archaeological work at any one place has been at Middleton Hall, first during restoration in the 1980s, as noted above. It continued during creation of the National Botanic Gardens in the 1990s, again in the early 2000s and then again in 2015, as a new phase of garden and landscape restoration was planned. A series of small excavations, watching briefs and building recording projects were undertaken during creation of the garden with two interlocking purposes, first to make a record of what was going to be destroyed or irrevocably altered, and second to inform the restoration process. The latter purpose is best exemplified at the double walled garden where identification of both the location and character of paths and other elements of the garden was possible, although it has not been possible to restore all the excavated features, such as the peach house constructed in about 1800.

Recent studies of Middleton Hall have focused on landscape archaeology - piecing together the history of the landscape and the estate from physical evidence, with particular emphasis on the site of the old hall which was constructed in the early seventeenth century and pulled down by William Paxton in the late eighteenth century during his remodelling of the estate. Low earthworks were identified as the site of the old hall in the 1990s. More recently it has been the subject of excavation by David Austin and survey by Louise Barker of the Royal Commission on the Ancient and Historical Monuments of Wales. Her survey shows just how much information can be gleaned from thorough examination of the landscape.

The site of the old hall is clearly defined but an expert eye is required to detect the location of formal gardens, terraces and ornamental ponds. In 2015, archaeological topographic survey of the picturesque landscape element of the estate by the Dyfed Archaeological Trust, in advance of restoration, identified previously unrecorded paths and viewpoints and will inform a programme of restoration. The Dyfed Archaeological Trust (then Cambria Archaeology) carried out a similar exercise at Dinefwr Park in 2003. Here, as well as identifying amongst other things picturesque walks and viewpoints, it was possible to demonstrate that many of the massive veteran oaks trees stand on flattened field boundary banks representing remnants of the agricultural landscape prior to the creation of a deer park in 1660. Parks like Dinefwr, in which mature trees were enclosed in their circuits, are called pseudo-medieval and are a recognised feature of the British landscape.

Aberglasney rivals Middleton Hall for the volume of archaeological work undertaken, but here it was in a much more concentrated area and over a shorter period of time, with the results summarised in a single volume. There had been a lot of debate concerning the date and function of some of the more enigmatic structures at Aberglasney, with the gatehouse and cloister garden being particularly controversial. Large-scale excavation around both these structures demonstrated their seventeenth- century origins and that they underwent considerable modifications. Most spectacularly, the excavations revealed a series of ornate cobbled paths, some of which it has been possible to incorporate into the restored garden.

Sources:

Avent, R., 1979. 'Laugharne Castle 1978', *Carmarthenshire Antiquary* 15, 39-56.

Austin, D. and Thomas, R., 2012. 'A garden before the garden: landscape, history and the National Botanic Garden of Wales', *Landscapes* 13, 32-56.

Blockley, K. and Halfpenny, I., 2002. *Aberglasney House and Gardens: Archaeology, History and Architecture*, British Archaeological Reports British Series, Book 334.

Brown, A. E., 1991. *Garden Archaeology*, Council for British Archaeology Research Report 78.

Dyfed Archaeological Trust, 2015. Archaeological topographic survey of Llyn Mawr and Llyn Felin Gat romantic landscape, unpublished report.

Evans. P., 2001. Middleton Hall, Carmarthenshire: Archaeological Excavation, Cambrian Archaeological Projects Ltd, unpublished report 167.

Evans, P. and Milne, H., 2001. Peach House Excavations 2001, National Botanic Garden of Wales, Carmarthenshire, Cambrian Archaeological Projects Ltd unpublished report 194.

Gallagher, 1987. The Bath House Middleton Hall Estate Interim Report unpublished.

Schlee, D., 2007. Excavation at the Cold Bath House, Dinefwr Park, 2007, Cambria Archaeology unpublished report 2007/74.

Allotments

J Holland

The history of allotments and the allotment
movement dates back to the social upheaval
of the enclosure of land by the large
landowners, and the dispossession of the
labourer from 1760 to 1845.

Allotments in Carmarthen 1950s (photograph: Richard E Huws)

ALLOTMENTS

The history of allotments and the allotment movement dates back to the social upheaval of the enclosure of land by the large landowners and the dispossession of the labourer from 1760 to 1845.

An allotment is a parcel or plot of ground generally divided into ¼ acre strips and rented to individuals to grow vegetables for their own use. The allotment movement gained momentum in the early nineteenth century during a period of economic and social crisis, and was an attempt to improve the living conditions of the poor. There were a number of contributory factors, including the war with France which ended in 1815 and the introduction of the Corn Laws. To reduce dependence on wheat and barley, the potato was promoted as a food staple. The growing of potatoes was also encouraged because the manuring of the land before planting enriched the land, and harvesting the potatoes prepared it for other crops. The temporary subletting of land to grow potatoes became common, the farmer ploughing and manuring the land, while the tenant provided his labour. The widespread adoption of the potato was followed in 1845 by potato blight, which resulted in greater deprivation amongst the agricultural poor.

 As early as 1608 William Vaughan of Golden Grove wrote of landlords: '*not content with such revenewes as their predecessours received nor yet satisfied that they live like swinish Epicures quietly at their ease, doing no good to the Commonwealth and do leave no ground for tillage, but do enclose for pasture many thousand acres of ground within one hedge, the husbandmen are thrust out of their owne, or else by deceit constrained to sell all they have. And so either by hook or by crook they must needs depart away, poore seely soules, men women and children*'.

Before land was enclosed there was a right to commons, land to graze geese, sheep, pigs and cattle, to collect firewood, and to cut gorse for burning. Without the right to pasture the peasant's only resource was his labour. As early as 1831 an Act of Parliament empowered church wardens and poor law overseers to supply up to 20 acres of land for the benefit of the labouring poor.

The loss of rights of common led to a greater dependence on poor relief and to a good deal of debate on how the burden of poor relief could be reduced. This led to many experiments in England and Wales on the provision of allotments. It was claimed that allotments would substantially reduce the amount of poor relief required. The question was how much land should be allotted without reducing the energy the labourer had to give to his main employment. It was often argued that the labourer working for himself would not have the time and energy left to labour for his master.

Allotments were provided by benevolent landlords, the church, the growing railway companies and the parish, with the aim of reducing the poor rate, helping the poor and encouraging the poor to stay on the land, to stem the flow of poor labourers to the growing towns. Land provided for allotments was generally marginal land, from old brickwork sites, quarries, and sites that were less suitable for development.

During the Victorian period allotments varying in size from 10-40 rods (40 rods is ¼ acre) were provided for the growing of vegetables, 1-4 acres as field allotments for growing wheat, barley and millet, potato patches for potatoes and beans, and cow runs (often operated on a communal basis). Cow runs were large enough not only to provide summer pasture, but also to provide sufficient hay to overwinter cattle.

In 1886 Lord Onslow, in Landlords and Allotments wrote: *'It is admitted on all hands that the poor man who has an allotment ungrudgingly bestows labour upon it, before and after his regular hours of work, and that the result of this additional labour both for his own and his family's part, is shown by a material improvement in his social as well as financial position. The farmers do not complain that labour bestowed on a small allotment is to the detriment of that for which they receive wages'.*

The Local Government Act (1894) established Parish and Urban Councils and gave them the responsibility to provide land for smallholding and allotments. The emphasis had changed from providing allotments to feed poor families, to allotments being held by artisans and tradespeople who lived and worked in the expanding towns. This happened in places like Llanelli that rapidly expanded to meet the demand for the production of coal and steel for the new industries.

The Royal Commission on Labour, 1894 reported that *'allotments are reported to be unpopular in Wales: potato grounds, however are to be found everywhere and gardens are very commonly attached to cottages'.*

 It was not until the First World War and then only after the passing of The Defence of the Realm Act (DORA, 1916) that the Carmarthenshire Council made any attempt to provide

Dinefwr Allotments (photograph: J Holland)

allotments. Lord Selbourne, President of the Board of Agriculture, encouraged the Boroughs and County Boroughs to produce as much food as possible from allotments and gardens, to help feed the country at war.

1917 saw a spate of reports in the local papers on meetings across the county to find suitable allotment sites in Ammanford, Crosshands, Coedmawr, Llanarthney, Llannon, Pontardulais and Tumble. In Pontardulais the Graigola Merthyr Colliery Co. took a lead in making arrangements to secure allotments for their employees. In Llandovery land for growing potatoes was advertised by a local farmer at one shilling for 20 yards of drill.

Land at Park Hall near Richmond Terrace, Carmarthen, was offered for the duration of the war. The Carmarthen Journal reported that: *'The Masters of the Carmarthen Grammar School and the pupils of the County Girls School are to be highly commended upon their untiring efforts in connection with their plots. The girls have devoted their gymnastic and games lessons to working in the school garden'.*

On 12 January 1917 it was reported in the Journal that a Mr K Walker had offered to plough the allotments in the park and to supply 120 loads of manure in exchange for 2 acres of land inside the cycle track in Carmarthen. *'Mr Jones said the feeling in Carmarthen was very much against the inside of the track being cut up. It had cost £2,700 for the cement track alone.'* They decided to offer Mr Walker another part of the park instead.

The Western Mail 26 March 1918 reported: *'Carmarthenshire County Council under the Smallholding and Allotments Act 1908 ... Notice is given hereby that the County Council for the Administrative County of Carmarthen propose to submit a compulsory order to the Board of Agriculture and Fisheries to enable them to hire compulsorily for a term of 35 years the fields of land numbered on the Ordnance Survey map 898 (part) 798,851,799,1003,1001,999,960,959,1005,1006.'*

In 1918 the Allotment Holders Association was created representing the Parcmain, Richmond Terrace, Priory Street, Old Grammar School and the Railwaymen's site. The Priory Street site was the largest at that time having 60 plots.

The Park allotments were closed after the war and were relocated in the lower part of the Lloyd's Field site (Five Fields). It was not until 1921 that the new Carmarthen Allotment Holders Society was formed. In December 1922 three sites, which had been procured under the 1908 Allotment Act, were handed over by the Council to the newly formed Allotment Society.

These were:
1. Five Fields rented from the Commissioners of Church Temporalities in Wales at a rent of £35 pa for a term of 14 years. This was later sold to the University of Wales in 1940 and to the Borough of Carmarthen in 1949.
2. Priory Allotment site on a 3 year lease at £12 pa from Jesus College, Oxford.
3. Half an acre leased from James Jones at an annual rent of £7.

The Allotment Society took over the running of the sites, set the rents and bought seed and plants in bulk to sell to members. They arranged an annual allotment and horticultural show and awarded a silver cup for the best allotment. Flowers were not to be taken into account by the judges.

Between the wars there was a decline in allotment holding. Land requisitioned for the war was returned to its former use. In 1932 The Old Grammar School site was closed. The displaced allotment holders were offered plots at the Priory site.

The 1925 Allotment Act encouraged local authorities to consider allotment provision as a vital part of their future town planning policy, and ensured that established sites purchased for that purpose would be protected by the need for ministerial permission before they could be disposed of, sold, or used for any other purpose. To this day the Priory Street and Five Fields sites still exist as allotments.

The onset of the Second World War in 1939 saw another big increase in the demand for land for allotments. On 4 October 1939 The Ministry of Agriculture launched the Dig for Victory Campaign. The aim was to get half a million new allotments into production as soon as possible. A series of Dig for Victory leaflets were published throughout the war, giving instructions on every aspect of growing fruit and vegetables. The local papers carried regular features on tasks to be done in the garden.

On 5 November 1943 the Minister of Agriculture, Mr R. S. Hudson, spoke at a meeting in Carmarthen. He said that the country was approaching world stringency in the food situation, and in view of this he appealed to every food producer to put forth still greater efforts.

After the Second World War there was a sharp decline in the number of allotment sites, and the need for new housing saw many sites across the country being developed. The Allotment Act of 1950 was the last major legislation on allotments and was aimed at securing tenure for allotment holders. Rationing continued until the mid 1950s but even food shortages failed to stop the loss of allotment sites. With greater prosperity by the mid 1960s almost 20% of allotment sites were derelict.

In more recent years allotments have again become popular, with the organic movement and a push to get back to nature. More and more people are taking to growing their own fruit and vegetables. With this resurgence in interest in allotment growing, there have been

Dinefwr Community Allotments
(photograph: J Holland)

a number of new reports, generated both by national and local government, looking at allotment provision in Wales. The Welsh Government commissioned a report on allotments in 2010, and on 17 February 2011 Carmarthenshire Policies & Resources Scrutiny Committee reported on the ongoing need for allotments in the county. It concluded that:: *'Allotments are increasing in popularity across the UK. Concerns regarding food origin and quality coupled with the current financial pressures are some of the main causes for increasing demand. Carmarthenshire County Council has received a number of requests since 2007 and the Council is responding by assisting in identifying suitable plots of land, where possible... suggestion of sub-letting of council tenants' gardens, would not only assist in providing additional plots of land for cultivation but would also have a positive impact on the aims and objectives of the local authority's Environment Works Project.'*

The allotment movement is still very much alive today. The National Trust opened a new site of 60 allotments in Llandeilo in 2009 and in 2012 Llannon community allotments were opened with a waiting list for the second phase.

In March 2013 Carmarthen Mayor Phil Grice said *'the allotments are the green lungs of the town and the more we can get the better that would be for Carmarthen. Firstly because it is good for the environment and secondly because it stops there being too much over development'.*

Dinefwr Community Allotments (photograph: J Holland)

Today there are nine allotment sites across Carmarthenshire. Carmarthen has two public sites: Five Fields off Monument Hill with 90 plots and Parc Hinds with 40 plots off Old Priory Road. Carmarthen also has 12 plots available to council staff at St David's Park. In Llanelli there are St Paul's Allotments, Bigyn Park Terrace with 26 plots, Coronation Road 17 plots, Lower Trostre Road 5 plots and Sunninghill Terrace with 24 plots. Kidwelly has one site, Cae Maliphant run by the Kidwelly Allotment Association (number of sites not reported). Llandeilo has one site at Home Farm, Dinefwr Estate provided by the National Trust with 60 plots and Llannon has a new site that opened in 2012.

The allotment movement, having begun as a means of feeding the poor and reducing the parochial poor rate in agricultural districts, has evolved over the last two hundred years and become part of the urban landscape. Today the allotment provides healthy exercise, contact with the land, and food for many city dwellers across the whole spectrum of rich and poor, old and young. The social history of allotment gardens forms a rich part of our cultural heritage. It offers healthy exercise and nourishment for generations to come.

Sources:

Carmarthenshire County Council Policy and Resources Scrutiny Committee, 2011. *Allotment Provision in Carmarthenshire..* Web. 18 September 2015.

Crouch, D. and Ward, C., 1997. *The Allotment: Its Landscape and Culture,* (Nottingham: Five Leaves Publications).

National Library of Wales Newspaper Archive.

Poole, S., 2006. *The Allotment Chronicles: A Social History of Allotment Gardening,* (Kettering: Silver Link Publishing).

Sustainability Committee, 2010. *Allotment Provision in Wales,* online. National Assembly for Wales, 20 September 2015.

Tiller, R., 2007. Allotment and Allotment Culture in South West Wales in the Twentieth Century' unpublished MA local history thesis, Trinity College Carmarthen.

Conserving Parks and Gardens

A Pyper

The large estates that once invested resources and labour into creating and maintaining an appropriate setting to their grand residences, have largely disappeared. The challenge of maintaining these large tracts of landscape falls to a multitude of individuals and organisations.

Dinefwr Park (photograph: M Ings)

CONSERVING PARKS AND GARDENS

Carmarthenshire is deservedly known as the Garden of Wales, rich in beautiful gardens and designed landscapes. However, it is a constantly changing and evolving landscape. The large estates that once invested resources and labour into creating and maintaining an appropriate setting to their grand residences have largely disappeared. The challenge of maintaining these large tracts of landscape falls to a multitude of individuals and organisations. Therefore gardens and parks vary immensely in their survival; some, like Dinefwr, are cared for and maintained, others such as Aberglasney have been recovered from obscurity to be restored. There are those rare examples like Middleton Hall, which continues to develop into the twenty-first century in a new direction as the National Botanic Gardens of Wales. There are, unfortunately, many which have seen a gradual decline over time as landscape priorities have changed.

The parks and gardens of Carmarthenshire are the product of various phases of design; or development over many years. A wide range of influences bear on their character and so when caring for the landscape it is important to recognise this dynamic and to understand their significant features and what gives them their essential character.

A park or garden might be important for many reasons, or for only one. These may include providing an appropriate setting for an important historic building; there may be associations with specific historic events, significant individuals or artistic endeavours; the site may have an archaeological or biodiversity value in its own right, or demonstrate a historic innovation or technological advance. Parks and gardens may demonstrate any of these factors, but they will also encapsulate a physical expression of artistic values, our forebears' relationship with nature, and the aspirations of their time.

There are many and varied threats, including the loss of features such as mature parkland trees and the decay of built features, or there may be the threat of encroaching development. Increasingly climate change is becoming a real concern bringing with it a changing environment and diseases or pests which may come to jeopardise key species and planting schemes.

The impacts of climate change on historic parks and gardens are difficult to assess as they will vary enormously according to the type of park of garden, and there will be positives as well as negatives. The most significant impacts will occur in unmanaged parks and gardens where trees and other plants lost to pests, diseases and storm damage will not be replaced, and the speed of degradation and erosion of 'hard' garden features will increase under more frequent storms. It is more likely that in managed parks and gardens these losses will be mitigated and their essential historic character retained.

In Carmarthenshire the loss of mature park trees is a key issue. With a high point of park creation in the nineteenth century, many of these parkland trees in the early twenty-first century are coming to the end of their natural lifespan and are often not being replaced. Most parks in the county are primarily agricultural land, and while they were almost always pastoral in use, increased pressure may now lead to agricultural improvement regimes including ploughing, which damages tree roots, and the application of fertilizer, which creates unfavourable conditions for parkland trees. In addition new farm infrastructure such as trackways and buildings may encroach unsympathetically upon the landscape.

Clearly, changing management priorities and lack of resources often lead to the neglect of built structures or features such as park walls and bridges, which suffer unless subject to routine maintenance. Likewise historic water features may become silted up or overgrown.

Just as much as neglect, misguided new works can also be detrimental to the park landscape, with inappropriate planting schemes or the introduction of unsympathetic new species. Conservation is about managing change, and understanding the character of what is to be conserved is fundamental to protecting a landscape. The principles of conservation lie in understanding the significance of all its elements, aesthetically, historically, culturally and ecologically as well as its historic landscape character.

In Wales, parks and gardens recognised to be of national importance are included in the *Register of Landscapes, Parks and Gardens of Special Historic Interest in Wales* compiled by Cadw. The Register was begun in 1992 and published in six regional volumes between 1994 and 2002, when the Carmarthenshire, Ceredigion and Pembrokeshire volume was published. A supplementary volume was published in 2007 and new sites are added and existing ones amended from time to time. In the same way as listing, parks are categorised as Grade I, II* or II. At the time of writing there are 19 registered parks and gardens in Carmarthenshire with Plas Dinefwr registered at Grade I, and Golden Grove, Aberglasney and Paxton's Tower at II*.

Developed as an advisory document to help with the conservation of historic parks and gardens in Wales, the register will now become a statutory document with the 2016

Historic Environment (Wales) Bill. Whilst it does not have any new planning or consent procedures, local planning authorities are expected to take into account the effect of a development on a registered site as a 'material consideration'.

The planting of new trees maintains the nature of the parkland (photograph: A Pyper)

The vast majority of parks and gardens are unregistered. A survey carried out in 2007 demonstrated that between Llangadog and Dryslwyn there were 24 individual parks which could be identified from nineteenth-century historic mapping, of which just three were registered: Dinefwr, Aberglasney and Golden Grove.

For owners and land managers wishing to develop their knowledge and understanding of historic parks and gardens there are a number of resources to help investigate the significant aspects of a historic landscape. Key organisations for accessing historic documents include the local Archives Service, the National Library of Wales, the Historic Environment Records held by the Dyfed Archaeological Trust, and the National Monument Record held by the Royal Commission on the Ancient and Historical Monuments of Wales. A wide variety of sources including historic maps, photographs, estate maps and sale catalogues all help build up a garden portrait and identify key elements.

Maintaining walls and railings
(photograph: A Pyper)

Advice and support is available at a local level through the Welsh Historic Gardens Trust and through the Heritage Management services at the Dyfed Archaeological Trust. Both these organisations are keen to raise awareness and understanding of the importance of parks and gardens, however large or small, whether they lie in urban or rural settings. They can provide practical advice and guidance to help owners, land managers and interested parties maintain and conserve this rich inheritance into the future.

Sources:

Cadw: Welsh Historic Monuments, 2002. *Register of Landscapes, Parks and Gardens of Special Historic Interest in Wales. Part 1: Parks and Gardens* (Cardiff: Cadw).

Pyper, A., 2007. An Assessment of the Historic Parks and Gardens in the Tywi Valley, Dyfed Archaeological Trust unpublished report.

Whittle, E., 1992. *The Historic Gardens of Wales* (Cadw). (London: HMSO).

Early Deer Parks

K Murphy

Deer parks were tracts of land, enclosed by wall, by a bank and ditch, or by a pale, set aside for deer and other wild animals to provide a food supply, for the management of woodland and to provide other resources such as stone or minerals.

Deer grazing in the distance, Dinefwr Park (photograph: J Holland)

EARLY DEER PARKS

There are about fifty medieval deer parks recorded in Wales, almost all of which are in the south-east of the country and in the Marches. There are a handful in Pembrokeshire, and only two known for certain in Carmarthenshire. Deer parks were tracts of land enclosed by wall, by a bank and ditch, or by a pale, set aside for deer and other wild animals to provide a food supply, for the management of woodland and to provide other resources such as stone or minerals. More importantly, deer parks were also a measure of status, as only the most wealthy could create and maintain them, as well as being the locus of recreation and leisure in the form of hunting, and consequently were usually within close distance of a castle or major house. One would expect most major castles - and there is no lack of them in west Wales - to have access to land for the hunt, and so the paucity of deer parks in the county is a little perplexing; it may be an indication that there was ample, readily available open land and deer for the chase and thus no need to build an enclosed park, unlike in the more intensively cultivated land in south-east Wales and along the Marches.

Aquatint of Dinefwr Castle and Park by Paul Sandby, 1777s showing a herd of deer (courtesy of the National Library of Wales)

Llansteffan is one of the two known medieval deer parks in the county. It was mentioned in documents from 1388 onwards, and probably located to the south-east of Llansteffan Castle around a farm still known as Lords Park. Records from about 1500 suggest deer were no longer kept and that the park was given over to agriculture. The exact location of the other medieval deer park in the county, associated with the castle at Newcastle Emlyn, is equally difficult to pin down. It is probably located to the south of the castle in the vicinity of a farm called Bwlch y Pal. Like the one at Llansteffan before the end of the Medieval Period, it no longer functioned as a deer park as John Leland in 1536-39 noted '*a park was there ons palid*'. Further research may reveal evidence of medieval deer parks associated with other castles, including those at Carmarthen Kidwelly, Llandovery and Carreg Cennen.

At the end of the sixteenth century Sir John Perrot transformed Laugharne Castle from a medieval fortress to a Tudor mansion suitable for an Elizabethan gentleman. As well as a modern house, Perrot wanted a deer park for '*the recreation of gentlemen*' and chose a site at Cyffig 8km north-west of the castle at the highest point of the Lordship of Laugharne. This was a park for hunting, very much in the medieval style, with none of the ornamental elements that were to characterise deer parks in the following centuries. Construction of the park in 1593 is well documented and is described in this volume under Laugharne Castle.

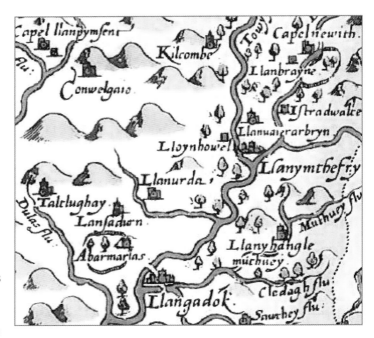

Extract from Christopher Saxton's 1578 map showing the deer parks at Glan Bran and Abermarlais.

Christopher Saxton depicts a deer park on his 1578 map to the east of Glan Bran house, the seat of the Gwynne family, in the north-east of the county. This park occupied a low hill and although long out of use and now under forestry and pasture fields, the boundary of its elongated oval shape can still be traced on maps and aerial photographs. Little is known about the origins and use of this park, although its location some distance from the house indicates hunting and the raising of game was its chief functions; this is supported by the presence of pillow mounds (artificial rabbit warrens) within the park.

Abermarlais is the only other deer park shown on Saxton's map. It was in existence by 1531 when it was described as paled, two-and-a-half miles in compass and well-wooded, and is shown on a 1761 estate map. By 1809 it was called the '*old Park*' and according to Richard Fenton '*appeared to have been well wooded by the old Stools*'.

Other deer parks in the county were of a different character from those at Llansteffan, Laugharne, Abermarlais and Glan Bran, having more emphasis on the ornamental than the sporting. Dinefwr is undoubtedly the best survivor. Long sections of the stone walls constructed in 1660 around this park survive and a herd of deer thrive in this National Trust owned property. Just across the Tywi valley from Dinefwr at Golden Grove a deer park was in existence from at least the early seventeenth century and in 1714 reference was made to '*the Old and New Parks*'. Remodelling of the parkland from 1830 onwards has obscured much of the earlier parks, although a herd of deer still live here. There are likely to have been other deer parks associated with great houses of the county, but references to them are tantalising thin, such as the sale particulars of Llangennech Park of 1820 that refer to *'an ancient deer park'*.

Sources:

Hearne, T., 1744. *The Itinerary of John Leland the Antiquary* (London).

Jones, F., 1987. *Historic Carmarthenshire Homes and their Families* (Carmarthen: Carmarthenshire Antiquarian Society).

Liddiard, R. (ed.), 2007. *The Medieval Park: New Perspectives* (Bollington: Windgather Press).

Murphy, K., 2009. 'Sir John Perrot's deer park at Cyffig'. In James, H. and Moore, P. (eds) *Carmarthenshire and Beyond: Studies in History and Archaeology in Memory of Terry James* (Carmarthen: Carmarthenshire Antiquarian Society) 231-34.

Pritchard, H. and Ings, M., 2015. Medieval and Early Post-Medieval Deer Parks, unpublished report by Dyfed Archaeological Trust, report no. 2015/18.

Rees, S., 1932. *South Wales and the Borders in the 14th Century*, map: south-west sheet.

Saxton, C., 1578. *Map of Radnorshire, Brecknockshire, Cardigan and Carmarthenshire.*

Deer grazing at Dinefwr Park (photograph: M Ings)

Icehouses

J Holland

The first use of icehouses or pits is very early, possibly Roman. There is mention of ice-pits during the medieval period, but icehouses were not introduced to Britain until the seventeenth century.

Dinefwr Icehouse (photograph: J Holland)

ICEHOUSES

Before the refrigerator was introduced in the early 1900s, food was restricted to what was available in season. To extend the season and to increase variety in winter, produce could be preserved in a number of ways. Meat and fish was preserved through drying, smoking and salting, while fruit and vegetables were preserved by pickling, bottling in syrup, or were made into jams and chutneys.

The first use of icehouses or pits is very early, possibly Roman. There is mention of ice-pits during the medieval period, but icehouses were not introduced to Britain until the seventeenth century. One of the first recorded icehouses was commissioned by James I at Greenwich Park in 1619.

By the late nineteenth century almost every large country house had an icehouse. Surviving examples can be seen in Carmarthenshire at Dinefwr, Golden Grove, Glynhir and Middleton. There were also icehouses at Bradbury Hall, Brynteilo, Dol-hardd, Edwinsford, Hafodneddyn and Plas Ystrad. Icehouses were not only used to provide ice for the house for culinary and medicinal purposes, but a few were used as a larder to store game, milk, and butter. Ice was taken up to the house by the outside staff and used in a cool room to chill dairy products and wines, and to make ice creams and deserts.

The construction of an icehouse consisted of four elements: an entrance, a passage, a chamber with a drain and a vaulted roof. They were often situated on the banks of a stream, above the groundwater level to facilitate drainage. Icehouses were either rectangular or circular. The most popular shape was that of a well, or egg standing on its end. They were sometimes constructed above ground with the earth banked in a mound around and above the ice chamber, or partly below and above ground level, or subterranean. A few were cut out of the bedrock. Earth was mounded over the entrance tunnel and storage chamber to provide insulation, and protection from the sun and rain. Some may have been thatched. Straw has long been used for its insulation properties, and for keeping out the rain. Many were situated at a distance from the house. The most elaborate had a structure built above them, in the form of a summer house or pavilion.

Where the site was exposed, the icehouse was built with flanking walls at the entrance to keep the sun off the entrance door. They were often located in shady places, usually close to the supply of ice, a pond or lake. Ice was cut in winter, loaded onto wagons, and taken to the icehouse where the ice was stored in layers of sawdust or straw to act as insulation. Winters were considerably colder than they are now, and where ice was not readily available snow was collected from the fields and compacted.

The passageway had up to four doors for added insulation. Many were straight but some were doglegged. Even passages were stuffed with straw, until the ice was needed, and the doors were sealed with leather, to prevent warm air entering the chamber. It must have been a chore to collect the ice for the house, to open each door, remove the close-packed straw, and chip out the required amount of ice from the solid mass below. The passage and chamber were brick lined with sloping floors to ensure good drainage into a channel, with a drain at the bottom.

By 1805 ice was being shipped in from Norway to meet demand. By the 1840s the demand for ice was so great that it was shipped from America. It was loaded on to trains and sent to estates all over the country. By the time it arrived at its destination almost 50% had melted. It was highly prized as clean ice, unlike that harvested from shallow lakes or ponds. Hard packed and well insulated ice would last anything up to 18 months, provided it was kept dry. The advent of refrigeration signalled the end of icehouses. Gradually in the nineteenth century icehouses became redundant, and now all are disused and mostly in a ruinous state.

Dinefwr
The largest icehouse in Carmarthenshire was probably that at Dinefwr which is 9m in diameter. It is recorded on the Ordnance Survey map, to the north of the house, amongst the trees. It is built against a north facing slope, and has been fully restored. It is partly subterranean, and partly above ground. The earth has been mounded around it. It has a short entrance passage which faces east, a brick lined domed vault and is topped with a stone-clad roof.

Golden Grove
The ice-house is situated in woodland to the west of the house. It is not shown on the Ordnance survey map. It was built of rubble stone and has largely collapsed.

The entrance to the icehouse at Dinefwr (photograph: J Holland)

Glynhir

The icehouse at Glynhir is a fine, well preserved example. It is constructed at the top of the valley, close to the house. It has a stone-lined passage which would have had three doors, and has a dog leg. Each section of the dog leg is about 3-3.5m long. It has a large subterranean chamber 4m in diameter with a domed roof and is 6m deep.

Middleton

Perhaps the best known icehouse in Carmarthenshire is the one at the National Botanic Garden of Wales (Middleton Hall), and can be seen across the field from the main broad-walk. It is cut into the slope immediately to the south-west of the double walled garden. It has a brick built, arched, entrance with a stone built splay either side, to keep the sun off the entrance door. It had thee wooden doors. The chamber is domed and brick lined. It is about 5m deep and just under 2m in diameter.

Sources:

Cadw: Welsh Historic Monuments, 2002. *Register of Landscapes, Parks and Gardens of Special Historic Interest in Wales. Part 1: Parks and Gardens* (Cardiff: Cadw).

Buxbaum, T., 2014. *Icehouses,* (Oxford: Shire Publications).

The entrance to the icehouse at National Botanic Garden of Wales (photograph: M Ings)

Walled Kitchen Gardens

J Holland

In Carmarthenshire there is scarcely a large house of significance without its walled garden.

The Wallace Garden, Middleton Hall, National Botanic Garden of Wales (photograph: J Holland)

WALLED KITCHEN GARDENS

In Carmarthenshire there is scarcely a large house of significance without its walled garden. These vary greatly in size and scale, from single walled enclosures like that at the Bishop's Park in Abergwili, to multiple walled enclosures like those at Aberglasney and Taliaris. Some have been lavishly restored and brought back into productive use like the double walled garden at Middleton Hall, and at Aberglasney, both of which are open to the public, while others have been grassed over or razed to the ground with only the outline of the walls remaining like that at Maesycrugiau.

Fruit trees over arches, Aberglasney (photograph: J Holland)

Enclosed kitchen gardens would have been surrounded by hedges, fences or walls. They were enclosed to keep out predators and thieves, and to protect tender or vulnerable plants from bad weather, particularly wind and frost. Walls absorb heat during the day, and release it overnight. They were also used as quiet places of contemplation and exercise. They combined the production of fruit, vegetables and herbs for the table with flowers and herbs for decoration, medicines, disinfectants, pesticides, perfumes and dyes for the household.

Kitchen gardens were square or rectangular at first, or designed to fit the available space, and were sited conveniently close to the house and the supply of water. As the fashion for gardens became less formal in the eighteenth century, kitchen gardens were moved from under the best windows of the house and placed out of sight, and at some distance to the house, often screened by a shelter belt of trees or the brow of a hill. The shelter belt also provided the walls with protection from the wind. As growing and plant requirements were better understood, they were also sited near the stables and a ready supply of manure.

If available, a south facing, sloping site with an open aspect was chosen, to maximise the benefit from the sun and to provide drainage. East-west walls became longer, and north-south walls shorter, to maximise the amount of wall available facing the sun, and benefiting from its warmth. Plants to crop early were placed against south facing walls, later crops against west facing walls, thus extending the growing season.

As forcing frames and greenhouse became popular and were installed against the south facing walls, the height of the walls increased to accommodate them, and to provide support for fan trained and espaliered fruit. Most of the walled gardens described in the *Cadw Register of Landscapes, Parks and Gardens of Special Historic Interest in Wales* have walls of

2.5 to 3 metres in height. Curving walls gave them added strength, so many walled gardens had rounded corners (e.g. Llwynywermod's likened to the shape of a playing card).

Walls were often made from local materials, using stone, cob or clom (earth), and capped to protect them from the rain. Brick was favoured by the end of nineteenth century, as it retained heat well and was easy to work with to create openings for flues and planting. Where rubble stone was used they were often lined with brick. Most of the surviving walled gardens in Carmarthenshire date from the nineteenth century and are built of rubble stone. Separate walled gardens were also built for nuts like walnuts, almonds and sweet chestnuts, and some as orchards.

At first the ground was laid out in a grid with raised or sunken beds, with channels between for access by the gardener, and for watering and drainage. The raised beds were retained with planks laid lengthways, medieval beds by wattle or low hedges of herbs, or box. Drainage ditches were often covered and made with stones, bricks and tiles or pipes, and where the land sloped, fed into a dipping pond or into a canal. The size of a walled garden generally varied from about one to four acres. Derwydd is an example of a large walled garden, with a sundial in the centre and a stone two-storey summerhouse built into its north wall.

Normally walled gardens were divided into compartments with narrow raised beds, to avoid the soil being trodden on while worked. Later, as seed drills began to be used in farming, beds became flatter and rows longer. Seed was no longer broadcast, but planted in neat rows. They were laid out in quadrants, and with wide borders around the base of the

Pleached trees form a centrepiece around the dipping pond, Middleton Hall (photograph: J Holland)

walls. Where the two axis paths met at the centre, they were often embellished with a sundial, fountain, or dipping pond.

The seventeenth century saw the introduction of oranges from Europe. Seedlings were picked and eaten in salads, while orange trees were grown in tubs, so that they could be stood outside during the summer and brought into the warm indoors to overwinter. The pineapple was introduced in the eighteenth century and the dessert grape, melon, fig and peach in the nineteenth century. From the 1600s onwards, the expansion of trade across the world saw the introduction of exotics, and new varieties of tender fruit and vegetables to be grown under glass.

One of the first nurseries was founded in Brompton Park in 1681 to meet the growing demand for new varieties and plants. The earliest seed catalogues began to appear in the 1700s. In the 1800s nurseries began to appear in Carmarthenshire. Prior to that the big

The Peach House in the Double Walled Garden, Middleton Hall, National Botanic Garden of Wales
(photograph: J Holland)

houses would have received catalogues and seed lists from the expanding nurseries in England. Their orders would have been delivered by train and mail coach, and from itinerant salesmen.

As demand increased so did the need to provide heat and protection for the new introductions. Pineapples required heat throughout the year to grow, cropping in their second or third year. Heat was initially produced by fermenting manure in a pit and covering it with glass frames. It was also found that the by-product from the tanneries, oak bark, produced heat over a long period - anything from three to six months - by the addition of fresh tan, or by mixing it to continue the fermentation process. Forcing pits were often constructed of timber, brick or stone, with rubble in the base topped with manure.

Walls may have been heated originally by kitchen chimneys, but once the kitchen garden was removed to a distance, other and more advanced methods of heating were required. Pits and frames heated by tan and manure were replaced by lean-to glasshouses heated by stoves or furnaces with hot air passed around the structure via flues built into their back walls. The need for light was not at first appreciated, so that orange trees and other exotics brought inside for the winter often suffered from the lack of light, and the fumes from the stoves.

Walls became taller to accommodate glasshouses with pitched roofs. The industrial revolution in the late eighteenth century brought improvements

Fireplace to provide heat for the walls, Middleton (photograph: M Ings)

in the production of glass and heat, with a range of glasshouses constructed from iron and timber. Steam briefly replaced the heat from smoke in flues, from boilers placed on the other side of the wall. Examples of pipework and boiler pits can be seen at Derwydd, Glynhir and at Gellideg.

The introduction of hot water pipes brought more even and clean heat to the glasshouse. The repeal of the glass tax in 1845 made glass more freely available. Few walled kitchen gardens by the end of the nineteenth century were without their heated glasshouses. They were able to supply the kitchens with a wide range of fruit and vegetables throughout the year. At Abergwili, Bishop Owen's daughter Gwenonwy recalled the greenhouses in the kitchen garden where '*very large and well cultivated pineapples and orchids were grown*'.

As space became a premium inside the walls, slip gardens developed outside the walls and were used for fruit bushes, peas and beans and potatoes that required more space. At Middleton Hall the walled garden had a double wall with a slip garden between the inner and outer walls, creating not one micro climate but two.

By the early nineteenth century the main entrance was often in the south wall to provide the best view of the garden on entering, and a view of the south facing glasshouses.

The kitchen garden continued to be a place for walking and pleasure. It was important that not only was the garden productive, but also decorative. Bare beds, which had been cropped, were hidden by fruit trees trained on wires, at a low-level as step-over, or as dwarfs, trained horizontally to provide a screen. Pretty borders of flowers were mixed with the fruit, vegetables and herbs. Bee houses, bee boles, dovecotes, trelliswork, sundials, statues, urns and ornamental fountains were included. Tunnels and pergolas were added to be both decorative and to provide support for fruit. Seats and arbours were added to provide shade and seating for the visitor.

The walled kitchen garden required a large staff of indoor and outdoor gardeners. The outdoor gardeners worked in the beds and borders, digging, planting, weeding, pruning, tying in, spraying, watering and cropping. The indoor gardeners worked in the glasshouses sowing, potting, tending the pineapples, grapes, melons, figs and peaches. Digging was done with a spade or mattock until the 1820s when steel tipped forks became available.

After the First World War the number of gardeners dwindled, and throughout the twentieth century many of the walled kitchen gardens fell into decline. Large country houses no longer employed teams of gardeners to maintain them, families decreased in size, and imports from around the world of fresh fruit and vegetables reduced the need to produce them at home. Gardens like those at Aberglasney and Middleton were only revived at the end of the twentieth century, with public funding. Although there are a good number of walled kitchen gardens in Carmarthenshire only those at Aberglasney and Middleton are currently open to the public. It is hoped that the walled garden at the Bishop's Park at Abergwili will be restored and opened to the public in the next few years.

Sources:

Campbell, S., 1996. *A History of Kitchen Gardening,* (New York: Random House).

Wilson, C. A., (ed.) 2010. *The Country House Kitchen Garden 1600-1950,* (Stroud: The History Press).

Lower walled garden, Aberglasney (photograph: J Holland)

Water

Elisabeth Whittle

How water was used, either in its natural state or manipulated into many varying forms, either for utilitarian use or for the delight of park and garden owners, or both, is the subject of this chapter.

Thomas Hornor's 1815 painting of a cascade at Middleton Hall (courtesy of the National Botanic Garden of Wales. Reproduced by kind permission of the Grant family)

WATER IN CARMARTHENSHIRE PARKS AND GARDENS

There is no shortage of water in Carmarthenshire, whether it comes from the skies or gathers into the county's great rivers and runs down to the sea. How this water was used, either in its natural state or manipulated into many varying forms, either for utilitarian use or for the delight of park and garden owners, or both, is the subject of this chapter.

Water in its natural state is a major defining characteristic of the county. This mostly takes the form of its rivers, the greatest of which is the Tywi. Running the length of the county, taking in tributaries such as the Dulais, the Cothi, the Gwili, the Gwydderig and the Brân, the river Tywi, twisting and turning through its wide valley, provides the scenic backdrop to several of the great parks and gardens of the county. From the sixteenth or seventeenth-century gazebo on top of the medieval castle of Dinefwr there is a spectacular view of the valley and river below. Sir Richard Colt Hoare, visiting Parc Dinefwr in 1793, stated that the river *adds much to the beauty of the surrounding scenery'*.

From Paxton's Tower (also called Nelson's Tower), built in 1808 as part of the Middleton Hall estate, there are spectacular views over the Tywi valley and conversely the tall building forms a prominent landmark above it. The early nineteenth-century landscaping at the Bishop's Palace, Abergwili, took advantage of the river by including a large pond which is an abandoned part of the river's course – an oxbow lake created in a flood in 1802. Sir Richard Colt Hoare noticed the river's loopy course: *'The river here takes a singular zig-zag course.'*

The Cothi is another river that plays its part in shaping the character of the county's parks and gardens. At Edwinsford the house is reached by a pretty arched bridge over the river, which is integrated into the surrounding gardens, providing beauty, movement and sound. Further upstream the river winds through the picturesque landscape park of Dolaucothi. Here the river has a history of its own. A 1770 map shows it flowing on a different course to today, its channel having been moved much closer to the house site. Subsequently it was removed back to its old course, also indicated on the map, where it remains.

Water runoff creates other natural features, such as ponds and waterfalls, which could be harnessed for utilitarian or ornamental use. The lakes at the medieval Talley Abbey, beautiful in themselves, would have provided the monks with an ample supply of fish. Waterfalls at Glynhir and Neuadd Fawr lent drama to the picturesque landscaping that was carried out in the nineteenth century.

The final natural element to consider here is the sea. Ornamental landscaping near the sea, on the estuaries of the great rivers, took full advantage of this watery backdrop, usually with buildings – belvederes, gazebos – which overlooked it. The prime example in the county is the gazebo at Laugharne Castle, built in the early nineteenth century (before 1830) on a raised terrace overlooking the estuary. It is said that in 1938 Richard Hughes wrote *In Hazard* here, fortifying himself for the task with the contents of the owners' wine cellar. At Gellideg a belvedere built in the early nineteenth century commanded extensive views not only of Carmarthen Bay but also of the Gwendraeth valley. The belvedere was later incorporated into the house. Terracing played its part:: from those at Iscoed there are fine views of the Tywi estuary.

Thomas Hornor's 1815 map of Middleton Hall estate (courtesy of the National Botanic Garden of Wales. Reproduced by kind permission of the Grant family)

The manipulation of water for utilitarian and ornamental purposes, often the two combined, dates back to at least the medieval period, when fishponds and water mills were much in use. Although much of the physical evidence has disappeared, archives from the Tudor period provide glimpses of how water was used. Abermarlais, in John Leland's survey of 1536-39, is described as '*a welle favored stone place motid'* : at this time houses were sometimes moated for both ornamental and useful reasons. At Laugharne Castle Sir John Perrot converted the castle into a mansion in the late 1580s, adding a '*proper fountaine'* in the inner court. Traces of this were found in excavations in the 1970s.

Ornamental pieces of water in the Tudor and Jacobean periods were generally formal, in the shape of pools or canals. The Tudor house at Golden Grove, built in 1560-65 by John Vaughan, lay in the Tywi valley below the present one in what is now the walled kitchen garden. This still contains a canal and lake, in existence by the mid seventeenth century and possibly contemporary with and associated with the Tudor house. Formal pools of this period are also found in the gardens at Aberglasney and Llechdwnni.

From the mid eighteenth century and through the nineteenth century the prevalent informality of landscaping led to the inclusion of naturalistic pools and lakes, sometimes complete with artificial features such as rills, weirs, cascades and even waterfalls, in parks and gardens. By damming whole valleys large bodies of water could be created. There are a few fine examples of such landscaping in the county, the outstanding one of which is Middleton Hall, now the National Botanic Garden of Wales.

Sir William Paxton returned a rich man from India and bought the Middleton estate in the late 1780s. He had grandiose ideas. Taking advantage of the natural rolling topography he laid out a fine landscape park, creating a water-dominated landscape with the help of a hydraulic engineer named James Grier. This fine landscape is beautifully recorded in Thomas Hornor's paintings of 1815. The main feature was a string of five lakes, on the largest of which Hornor depicted an elegant sailing vessel, clearly for the delight of visitors. With the lakes went seven bridges, some grand, some modest; artificial cascades and waterfalls in various sizes and styles, a grotto and bath houses. Paxton was interested in water management and intended to turn Middleton into a public spa. Although this never happened the 1824 Sale Particulars give an indication of Middleton's watery delights, now

Geraniums, kniphofia and lilies at the pool in the sunken garden at Aberglasney (photograph: N McCall)

Bath House at Middleton Hall painted by Thomas Hornor in 1815
(courtesy of the National Botanic Garden of Wales. Reproduced by kind permission of the Grant family)

long gone. They describe a *'rustic building'* with *'a chalybeate* [impregnated with iron] *spring, which has pipes, conducting the overflow to the outside of the Park'*. There was also a bath house *'the interior … adapted as a plunging bath; and also a hot bath, with Furnace Room'*.

Similar, but less ambitious, landscaping took place at other sites in the county. At Llwynywermod (formerly Llwynywormwood) George Griffies-Williams created a fine landscape park to go with his new mansion from 1785 to 1809. Below the house the valley of the Nant Ydw was dammed to create a lake of three and a half acres, which would have greatly enhanced the park's appearance. The earthen dam at the west end survives but at present the lake is drained. Water can be still, as in lakes, but it can also move and make sounds. These attributes were also brought into play at Llwynywermod where drives were led over bridges below which streams rippled and gurgled over stony cascades, possibly artificially enhanced. This is also the case at Stradey Castle where, in the nineteenth century, the Afon Dulais, which runs through the park, was picturesquely landscaped with bridges, weirs, lakes, including a skating pond, and a stepped cascade.

Parc Dinefwr contains the remains of a rare cold bath (Middleton Hall and possibly Taliaris also had them). Cold baths – small buildings with a cold-water plunge pool – became fashionable in the eighteenth-century but declined thereafter, perhaps due to lack of hardiness. The remains, by a spring on the west side of the park, were excavated in 2007, when the footings of the building and pool were found, together with fragments of marble suggesting a marble lining to the pool. The pool is known to pre-date 'Capability' Brown's visit in 1775, when he mentioned it. Interestingly, the spring was later harnessed to power two hydraulic ram pumps, the later one of which interfered with the structure of the cold bath, which fed water to a cistern above, from which the house was supplied.

Two sites in the county exemplify the many ways in which water has been harnessed, both for ornamental and utilitarian purposes – Glynhir and Taliaris. The river Loughor (Llwchwr), whose source is one of the natural wonders of Carmarthenshire, flows from north to south through a wooded valley at Glynhir. On the ornamental side, a dramatic waterfall became the main destination of picturesque walks in the early nineteenth century and a gently curving canal in the garden enhanced the setting of the house. On the utilitarian side a complex system of water management was instigated, also in the nineteenth century. Water from the river was fed via leats to ponds, the canal and to a Pelton wheel (in common use between 1870 and the First World War) in a stone structure to the north of the house. Through a system of wheels, cups, long wire and shaft the flow of water powered a range of agricultural machines.

Taliaris has an ancient pedigree. Its early landscaping was formal. When Edward Knight visited in 1760 he saw a *'small garden in the old taste & strait canal'*. There is now no trace of the canal. In 1785 (Sale Particulars) there were four fishponds, a fishing boat and a boat house. Tantalisingly, in 1840 a *'cold bath grove'* north of the house is mentioned, implying the presence of a rare cold bath. By this time there is only one piece of informal water in the park, Llyn Taliaris, and this is where the boathouse, in precarious existence, remains. The utilitarian features date to after 1833, when the property was bought by Robert Peel, cousin of Sir Robert Peel. They lie to the west of the house, where a header pond, leats and pipes feed water to a water mill and sawmill. It appears that this is the only example of a shaft-turbine, water-powered sawmill in Wales.

Waterspout at Aberglasney (photograph: J Holland)

Water in the county's parks and gardens runs the whole gamut of styles and uses and was harnessed from the medieval period, possibly earlier, right up to the present day to provide power, food, boating, bracing dips, skating, beautiful sights and sounds. The county's parks and gardens would be the poorer without it.

Cart-washing pond at Gellideg
(photograph: J Holland)

Dipping pool, Stradey Castle
(photograph: J Holland)

Aberglasney

J Atkin

The Tywi valley is an area of great historical interest, its margins punctuated with remains of ancient castles. Despite being one of the great house and gardens of the area for many centuries, Aberglasney had by the 1990s fallen into disrepair.

Aberglasney gatehouse and mansion in the snow (photograph: N McCall)

ABERGLASNEY, Llangathen (SN580221)

Aberglasney stands just over 60 metres above sea level, nestled in the saddle between two hills on a ridge overlooking the Twyi valley to the south. Grongar Hill, the higher of the two, and with an Iron Age hill fort, lies to the west. The Tywi valley is an area of great historical interest, its margins punctuated with remains of ancient castles. Despite being one of the great house and gardens of the area for many centuries, Aberglasney had by the 1990s fallen into disrepair. All that stood of the Cloister Garden were the gravity-defying remains of stone walls, bound together by dense vegetation that smothered their entirety. The once well-cultivated gardens were swamped with rampant invasive vegetation. An upper storey of self-sown ash and sycamore trees populated the grounds and specimens grew out of every conceivable crevice in the masonry. It is understandable why it was considered by most, quite literally beyond restoration and 'A Garden Lost in Time'.

The exceptional concept of saving and possibly restoring the crumbling structures at Aberglasney was initiated and driven by one man, William Wilkins, the visionary not only behind Aberglasney, but also the National Botanic Garden of Wales at Middleton Hall. In 1993 correspondence was exchanged between William Wilkins and Frank Cabot, the founder and Chairman of The Garden Conservancy based in New York, and a brilliant garden-maker. William Wilkins enclosed an article about the historical importance of Aberglasney. His curiosity aroused, the following year Frank Cabot, with his wife, Anne, made their first visit to Aberglasney to see for themselves the imminent disappearance of over four hundred years of history. The foresight and dogged enthusiasm of William Wilkins and the conviction, vision and remarkable philanthropy of Anne and Frank Cabot were magical ingredients. Their legacy is what can be seen today.

Aberglasney Restoration Trust was set up in May 1994. Experts of every kind were summoned, and funding was obtained from various sources. A vast project of clearance, evaluation and rebuilding began three years later. By 1999 the garden was being opened to the public and was appropriately entitled *Aberglasney: A Garden Lost in Time*. It would perhaps be more accurate to say the garden at Aberglasney was *found* just in time for restoration to save it. Today Aberglasney is both old and new. The famous Nine Green Gardens of Aberglasney have been resurrected and much of the precious architecture restored to its former glory.

Some fifteen years after opening, the restoration and equally important maintenance of the architecture and gardens continues in earnest. The site is now a nationally important piece of heritage and the gardens have recently been judged to be one of the top ten formal gardens in the UK by the Royal Horticultural Society (RHS). Today the gardens consist of far more than just the nine green gardens of old. The cloister range is now generally accepted to be an authentic example of a typical garden structure dating back to the early seventeenth century and is considered to be the only one that remains in the UK. Nearby there is now a fully restored ornate diaper-patterned path, which was contemporary with the building of the cloister range. The gatehouse at the end of the diaper path is preserved and the ancient yew tunnel has been restored to its former glory.

Elsewhere the upper and lower walled gardens have been restored. The upper walled garden has been designed to reflect the history of Aberglasney through a formally laid out Celtic cross. The design was the work of the famous garden designer Penelope Hobhouse and the garden is affectionately known amongst the gardeners as the 'Hobhouse garden'. The lower walled garden is set out in a similar cruciform fashion and is a traditional kitchen garden. Food and flowers are grown and harvested for the visitors' enjoyment with one part even doubling as a trial area for the RHS.

On the hill above the house an extensive woodland and bridged ravine garden has been created. This area is truly 'a plantsman's paradise'. Filled with exquisite rarities, mainly from Asia and North America such as *Shortia, Trillium* and *Cardiocrinum*, this area is something of a tribute to the great plant hunters of Victorian times. Nearby the planting palette changes to mainly woody plants in the Asiatic garden with a viewing point that allows Merlin's Hill to be seen in the distance. Also above the house is the alpinum, a rock garden of fair size. As expected the alpinum boasts many rarities and a multitude of different bulbous plants from all over the world.

Upper garden, Aberglasney (photograph: N McCall)

Below the house and cloisters the pool garden has been restored and offers a much more minimalist feel. A large rectangular pool fed by rills from ancient field drains that actually run under the mansion takes centre stage with Grongar Hill in the background. Below the pool garden a bulb meadow and stream garden can be found before the beginnings of Pigeon House Wood. This wonderful wooded area is home to a sea of wood anemones and bluebells. Unlike the rest of the garden this area is more managed than manicured, allowing native plants to take centre stage.

Following all the sterling work of the early restorations the gardens have not stood still; in fact they have continued to gallop forward. Generous donations have continued and piece by piece the gardens and mansion have developed even further. The challenge of further weather-proofing the visitor experience has been achieved with the addition of an award winning Ninfarium. This indoor garden was inspired by the ruined pleasure gardens of Ninfa and is a truly unique space and constant surprise to guests.

Elsewhere there have been further additions, such as a rose garden and arbour linking the cloisters with the gardens above the mansion. A more contemporary sunken garden with a courtyard feel has been created in part of the old home farm estate. This area also boasts a water feature designed by the famous William Pye. A generous donor has helped see the old aviaries restored. These wonderful buildings will soon be used to house a living time-

The Yew Tunnel (photograph: N McCall)

line of gardens through six centuries which feels like a very appropriate use considering Aberglasney's rich history.

Today the entire ground floor of the mansion and the famed staircase have been restored. This has added a much needed indoor attraction that also allows for art and craft exhibits. The ornate panelling that once adorned the great hall's walls has been reinstated. The intricate cornicing throughout the ground floor has been painstakingly

Bishop Rudd Bridge
(photograph:z N McCall)

restored. Visitors can also enjoy the wonderful plasterwork on the ceiling of the great hall which, combined with the cornicing and staircase, makes a spectacular sight.

Piece by piece the mansion at Aberglasney has been brought from the near irreversible ruin back to its former glory. This last piece of work is the fifth phase of restoration of the mansion and has finally brought it to a state where visitors can truly enjoy it for what it was in years gone by. The upper floors are still in need of restoration but from time to time visitors can enjoy tours of the upstairs and see the bare history that still remains. Most importantly, through the hard work of the Trust the mansion is now not only up and running but more importantly safe and available for people to enjoy.

More recently the Trust purchased further land which comprised another piece of the old home farm and a rather wet piece of woodland. This area being completed in Queen Elizabeth's Jubilee year turned out to be a much bigger project than was first planned. By mid 2012 a woodland bog garden had been created with huge borders containing drifts of exotic wet land plants. This sweeping area now links the pool garden with Pigeon Wood and offers a very different type of garden and planting to the others.

Aberglasney (photograph: N McCall)

It is not only the large projects that make the gardens; the ongoing small scale development of the gardens is as big a contributor as any of the larger projects. The wonderful collection of magnolia continues to be added to as do the collections of other plants that enjoy the Tywi valley climate. In recent years bulb displays have become a great part of the garden calendar and today between twenty and fifty thousand bulbs get planted every year. Most of these are permanent additions packing the gardens with interest from January to June.

Snowdrops, tulips and our nationally cherished daffodil are used throughout the gardens. In fact the daffodil collection is numbering nearly five hundred different types. Elsewhere in the gardens arches and arbours are being built in to create seasonal displays with plants such as roses, wisteria, and ornamental apples. Great care is taken in tastefully improving the colour schemes and visitors' journeys through the gardens so that the wonderful structures can also be enjoyed with either the plants or the architecture taking centre stage.

A current development is also the largest in the last seven years and this project is fondly named the piggeries. This unglamorous title refers to one part of the project which is the restoration of the old pigsties, there is however far more to the project. As mentioned the

Trust recently purchased another piece of land which contained the piggeries, a cow barn and cow sheds. These buildings are to be restored with further essential works to the services of the gardens included. The future use of these buildings will be as glasshouses, potting sheds, work rooms and mess rooms for the gardeners.

One of the motivations behind this choice is the recent successes the Trust has had with students and training in the gardens. Due to the need for better facilities for the volunteers and team as a whole, the old home farm buildings will be brought back into working order. The traditional practices of self-sufficiency will return. This project has also allowed for the conversion of some currently owned barns into student accommodation. The most senior gardener in the team also mentioned 'that we really are going back to the good old days'. By this he referred to the gardeners living on site, the growing of our own food and the use of locally produced fuel for biomass energy. This was a very apt description as part of the mission for the piggeries is not only the restoration of heritage but also the conservation of skills, tradition and the reinstatement of the working practices of a heritage garden.

After all the fine work restoring Aberglasney to its former glory, great care has been taken in developing the correct mind set or ethos for how the estate is kept and managed. As the house and garden have such architectural significance every care is required to keep them in the right manner. Aberglasney also boasts examples of heritage from different periods and different styles - for instance the Mansion areas are Victorian whereas the cloisters are much older. From a gardener's point of view this creates different challenges and on greater investigation one realises the deeper complexities of what is required.

One very interesting part of Aberglasney's history is that it was built before gardens as we know them had been invented. At the time of the cloisters, gardening for aesthetics was rare as most were more functional. The term garden usually meant fruit, vegetable or medicinal gardens. Gardens designed purely for aesthetics or art were very rare at this time in this area.

Today we aim to garden in the same spirit of days gone by. The emphasis is on horticultural excellence with innovation that is

Clivia in the Ninfarium, Aberglasney, (photograph: N McCall)

Aberglasney in about 1870
(photograph: courtesy Carmarthenshire Museum)

sympathetic to the heritage. We try to allow the garden to evolve and develop rather than remain static. We aim to honour the great vision of all the early owners of the gardens but also continue in the spirit of the more recent contributors such as Frank Cabot.

So with all these various elements taken into consideration our current ethos is to be 'A Heritage Garden of Excellence'. Ironically the head gardeners of previous times would probably have been given a very similar instruction by the owners of Aberglasney. This thought provides great comfort as it shows that despite all the years and restoration the traditions and goals of the site have not really changed.

Aberglasney is a Grade II* Registered Historic Park and Garden.

Abermarlais

K Murphy

Abermarlais is included in this gazetteer on account of being one of the oldest and longest lived parks and gardens recorded in Carmarthenshire.

Extract from the 1761 Abermarlais map (courtesy of Carmarthenshire Record Office)

ABERMARLAIS, Llansadwrn (SN692295)

Abermarlais is included in this gazetteer on account of being one of the oldest and longest lived parks and gardens recorded in Carmarthenshire. It has not fared well, the house has gone and with it the formal gardens and parkland; woodland, part of a walled garden, some paths and outbuildings survive attesting its former glory.

Francis Jones has researched and published the history of Abermarlais and its families, although little about the park and garden has found its way into print. At the time of writing the large collection of documents in Carmarthenshire Record Office relating to Abermarlais was not available, and so no original research was possible when compiling this gazetteer. For this reason and because the park and garden is now in such poor condition only a brief entry is provided.

Abermarlais is first mentioned in the early thirteenth century when it was in possession of Ednyfed Fychan, but it is not until a survey of 1531 that detail is available. Then it was recorded that the house with a gatehouse was moated and the park was paled, two-and-a-half miles in compass and well wooded, with a wood called Nether Forest nearby. John Leland, also in the 1530s, left a brief account of Abermarlais describing the house as being repaired and extended by Sir Rhys ap Thomas in the early sixteenth century. Sir Rhys had a passion for hunting, and it is thus possible that he established the park as part of his general improvements to the estate.

Interestingly, a kiln that produced bricks characteristic of the Tudor period was discovered close to Abermarlais during construction of a gas pipeline in 2008. It is tempting to suggest that these bricks were manufactured for Sir Rhys's improvements, possibly for his extension, which would make Abermarlais the only brick building of the period in the Tywi valley, indeed the only brick building in the valley between the Romans and the coming of the railways in the mid-nineteenth century. However, Leland describes the house as *'a well favorid stone place'*, so perhaps we need to search elsewhere in the neighbourhood for a Tudor brick building. Abermarlais house and the paled park is shown on Christopher Saxton's map of 1578. This park is one of two depicted by Saxton in Carmarthenshire, the other one being at Glan Bran in the north-east of the county.

It is not known what happened to the house and grounds over the following couple of centuries. In 1795 the estate was sold to Admiral Sir Thomas Foley. He immediately implemented changes, pulling down the old house and building a new one 150m to the west, and planting woodland. We are fortunate in having a map originally drawn in 1761 and now in the Carmarthen Record Office that documents these changes. This map is a true palimpsest, as not only does it show the 1761 estate and in a cruder hand Foley's changes, but faint, ghostly drawings of people and horses can be made out, perhaps done by a child. The deer park is outlined in green on the map as surveyed and drawn in 1761, labelled 'Park' with an area of 233¼acres and is shown on hilly ground lying to the north and north-west of the house. According to the map it was treeless. The house, in plan a courtyard, overlooked a bowling green to the south-east and a formal garden to the south-west with a rectangular walled garden beyond and outbuildings, including a barn to the south. Orchards and woodland are shown close to the house. A public road ran to the south-west of the gardens, separating them from what was probably parkland. Richard Fenton who visited in 1809 left a description of Abermarlais: '*Went through the old Park of Abermarlais, which appeared to have been well wooded by the old Stools, and to have been planted in Rows near the House, which had a bowling Green before it, and a piece of Water. The Admiral's young plantations amazingly thriving*'.

The changes shown on the map, which are dated as taking place between 1797 and 1812, include the relocating of the public road outside the estate boundary (now the route of the A40), the new house (shown in elevation not plan) and much tree planting, both in the deer park and around the new house, creating a parkland landscape in keeping with late eighteenth/early nineteenth century taste. It is assumed that the gardens accompanying the old house were erased as they are not shown on the 1887 Ordnance Survey 1:2500 First Edition map. This map shows the park and garden in its full Victorian glory, with the new house with its terraces and gardens sitting within wooded parkland and a walled garden some 250m to the north of the house. The old deer park is shown divided into fields.

Admiral Sir Thomas Foley's house at Abermarlais prior to its demolition
(photograph courtesy of Carmarthenshire Museum)

Abermarlais old postcard (courtesy P Davies)

All traces of the 'old' house and its gardens have been thoroughly wiped from the landscape, with just hints of the former moat visible on aerial photographs. The 'new' house has now been demolished. Its gardens were erased and the site is used for storage. The deer park stone boundary wall survives for much of its length. The park itself is a mixture of agricultural land and coniferous forestry, and the walled garden, whose walls are well-preserved, is a caravan park. Some surviving outbuildings have been converted to domestic use, and a lodge remains. The areas of woodland planted by Foley around his house do, however, survive, but with very little original planting, most trees being second or third generation re-growth, and his plantations in the old deer park have largely gone.

Sources:

Carmarthenshire Record Office, Glasbrook Add 1 – Exact Map of Abermarlais Demesne in ye Parish of Llansadwrn, Carmarthenshire, Surveyed and Mapped by I Davies 1761.

Fisher, J. (ed.), 1917. *Tours in Wales (1804-1813) by Richard Fenton* (London: Cambrian Archaeological Association).

Jones, F., 1967. 'Welsh Interiors: 2. Abermarlais', *Archaeologia Cambrensis* 114, 165-91.

Ammanford Park

K Arblaster

Ammanford Park was laid out in 1935 on a field of 10 acres called Cae Drud, which was originally part of Tirydail Farm on the Dinefwr Estate.

Postcard of Ammanford Park (courtesy of T Norman)

AMMANFORD PARK (SN 627123)

Ammanford Park was laid out in 1935 on a field of 10 acres called Cae Drud, which was originally part of Tirydail Farm on the Dinefwr Estate. The field name translates as 'precious field'. In the early 1900s this field was rented by the owner of the Cross Inn Hotel who encouraged its use for all kinds of sports including horse racing.

Ammanford, the third largest town in Carmarthenshire, came under Llandeilo Rural District Council until 1903. When the town became autonomous there were many things deemed more important than public spaces, so in 1914 the Ammanford Recreation Grounds Ltd. was formed by a group of residents, who raised money and took over the lease of Cae Drud – the Cricket Field, as it was then known.

The War intervened and it was not until 1920 that the Ammanford Urban District Council tried to negotiate to buy the Cricket Field from Lord Dynevor. They were only able to borrow £2500 through government schemes and Lord Dynevor would not reduce the price from £3081, so in 1923 they bought the land through a levy of 4d on the general rates – a huge increase at that time.

It took another three years for the boundary to be fenced, and it was not until 1934 that the full plans for the Park were executed. A local surveyor, J Owen Parry, laid out the grounds for the development scheme. The money, raised partly through a Public Subscription Fund, meant that a bandstand, miniature golf putting course, children's playground, pathways and tree planting could be added to the bowling green, tennis courts and cricket field. The Park was officially opened by Lord and Lady Dynevor on 14 May 1936.

The ornamental gates at the Iscennen Road entrance to the Park were also designed by J Owen Parry. They were erected in 1937, and paid for by the British Legion as a memorial

The bandstand (photograph courtesy of Carmarthenshire Museum)

for local men killed in the Great War. Cadw listed these Memorial Gates and the bandstand as Grade II in 1994.

Old postcard of the Memorial Gates, Ammanford Park (courtesy T Norman)

Sources:

Locksmith, W. T. H., 1999. *Ammanford: Origin of street names and notable historical records* (Carmarthen: Carmarthenshire County Council).

Ammanford Park (photograph: A Adams Rice)

Bay's Hill

H Whitear

The garden encompasses about an acre of
land, and the area appears to have been
used as productive gardens throughout the
nineteenth century.

Bay's Hill crenelated garden wall (photograph: H Whitear)

BAY'S HILL GARDEN, Llandeilo (SN630223)

Bay's Hill house and garden lie in the centre of Llandeilo on the north side of the churchyard of St. Teilo's church. Despite its central position in the market town, the site has avoided development and the garden and house are now rented out as holiday accommodation. The garden encompasses about an acre of land, and this area appears to have been used as gardens throughout the nineteenth century - it is shown on a map of 1826 divided into small squares. The same map shows a similar arrangement on land on the south side of Bridge Street, an area historically used as productive gardens for the town.

At its southern end, the ground level inside Bay's Hill garden is considerably higher than the ground level in the street (which forms the northern boundary of the churchyard). Here the garden is retained by a 3.5m high stretch of crenelated walling listed by Cadw (Grade II) as being of random rubble stone, with arched recesses, a broad cambered-head archway to the right (east) end, and a narrower elliptical-headed archway at the left (west) end. There is a small square rubble building on top of the wall above the left hand archway, with a slate roof and a narrow ogee-headed window. The wall was built in about 1840, and is described as being in the Gothic style.

This fantasy gothic appearance has almost certainly contributed to rumours that the garden *'is in fact the original site of Talley Abbey which we are told was located in the garden under the Yew tree'*. The assertion appears to be supported by historic Ordnance Survey mapping, which shows the site of a chapel within the garden. The Royal Commission on the Ancient and Historical Monuments of Wales records that in 1913 a local person remembered traces of a ruined building which, according to local tradition, once belonged to Talley Abbey. At this time the area around the chapel site was reportedly known as 'Cae Ysgubor Abad' (Field of the Abbot's Barn). The track that runs down towards the river from the end of Abbey Terrace is still labelled 'Ysgubor Abad' on modern Ordnance Survey maps, and may have originally defined the southern boundary of *'Cae Ysgubor Abad'* before the development of Crescent Road in the mid nineteenth century. The garden's proximity to the churchyard does suggest possible ecclesiastical associations, and in fact the Premonstratensian Abbey of Talley held land in Llandeilo during the medieval period. The name 'Cae Ysgubor Abad' could recall ownership of the site by the abbey, and perhaps the former existence of a barn on the site for collecting produce by the abbey authorities. If this site was abandoned sometime after the Dissolution of the Monasteries in 1536, a large barn in a ruinous state could have given rise to the idea that these were the remains of a chapel or abbey.

Buildings are depicted in this area on a *'Plan of the Town of Llandeilo and Lands 1826'*, which pre-dates the construction of the current Abbey Terrace. The medieval town of Llandeilo occupied the area around the churchyard, the marketplace, Bridge Street, and the lower part of Rhosmaen Street. Abbey Terrace would have formed part of the original road system around the churchyard along with King Street, Church Street and Bank Terrace.

The constant flow of horse and cart traffic would explain the height difference between the land behind the garden wall and the road below.

Bay's Hill crenelated garden wall
(photograph: H Whitear)

The construction of the road through the centre of the churchyard (1840s) ensured that Abbey Terrace was no longer a busy thoroughfare, and probably allowed for its gentrification. The current houses of Abbey Terrace are dated 1840 (a 'well-designed terrace of four', with Bay's Hill House at the right hand end, adjoining the crenelated stretch of wall).

It perhaps suited the occupants of these grand new houses to encourage recollections of the association with Talley Abbey, an association which may have lent itself favourably to the gothic design of the crenelated wall, whose construction in 1841 would have been a very imposing and visible symbol of the wealth, associations, taste and status of the owners of Bay's Hill. It would also have screened the private garden from the gaze of parishioners making their way into church.

Many specimen trees still dominate the garden and lend it a wooded appearance. These are likely to be survivals from the garden's Victorian phase, immediately after the construction of the wall, along with other Victorian garden features.

Sources:

Carmarthenshire Record Office, Whitehouse and Derwydd Estate Book by Wm. Goode, Plan of the Town of Llandeilo and Lands 1826.

Cadw listed building description : 11031 – Stretch of Walling & Archways between Nos. 5 & 7 Abbey Terrace, Llandeilo.

Llandeilo Fawr Parish Tithe Map, 1841.

www.llandeilo.org Llandeilo Town website

www.bayshillhouse.com Bays Hill House website

The Bishop's Palace Park

K Murphy

The Bishop's Palace Park is a fine example of early to mid-nineteenth century parkland, retaining much of its character as laid out by Bishop Murray and Bishop Jenkinson and containing elements from an earlier period of landscaping.

Aquatint of the Bishop's Palace Park (courtesy of Carmarthenshire Museum)

THE BISHOP'S PALACE PARK, Abergwili (SN441209)

The Bishop's Palace Park is a fine example of early to mid-nineteenth century parkland, retaining much of its character as laid out by Bishop Murray and Bishop Jenkinson and containing elements from an earlier period of landscaping.

The Bishop's Palace was in the hands of the Bishops of St Davids from the 1280s until 1972. It originated as a college of canons. The collegiate buildings were converted into a Bishop's Palace when the college was transferred to Brecon in 1541, and in 1972 the Bishop's Palace became Carmarthenshire County Museum when a new Bishop's Palace was built in the western portion of the grounds.

Documentary sources record a bowling green in the seventeenth century and a '*best court*' in 1713, but the creation of the park belongs to four main phases: the eighteenth-century '*pleasure grounds*' and garden; the laying out of a '*romantic*' landscape park by Bishop Murray (1801-1803); the creation of the present park by Bishop Jenkinson between 1829 and 1840; and the division of the grounds and construction of the New Bishop's Palace. Unlike family estates where preservation and curation of their ancestors' landscapes and buildings provided physical manifestation of right of possession and continuity across generations, at the Bishop's Palace new bishops seemed almost compelled to put their stamp on the landscape, changing or even erasing the work of their predecessors.

Old postcard of the Bishop's Palace (courtesy of P Davies)

A map of 1796 shows the pleasure grounds to the east of the house, a garden formerly a bowling green to the north, the *'Palace Yard'* to the west, a hay yard and outbuildings to the south and an open kitchen garden to the south-west. Some, if not all, of these elements were in place by 1750 when they are depicted on two paintings now in the British Library.

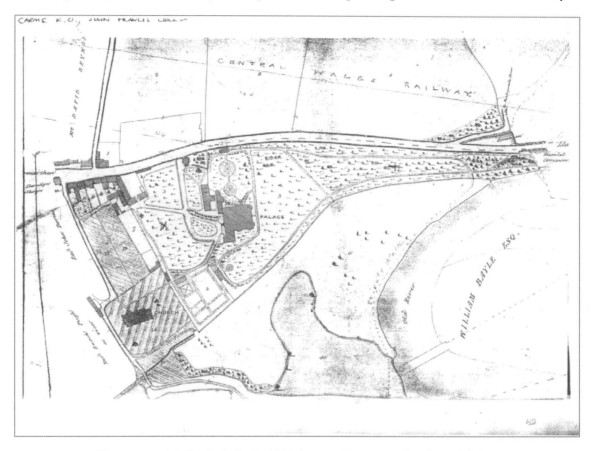

Estate map of the Bishop's Park, 1843 (courtesy Carmarthenshire Record Office)

The paintings show the treeless pleasure grounds with shrubs and espalier trees against walls. A ha-ha with ornamental wooden fence and wooden revetment separates the park from the wider landscape. It is unclear which Bishop was responsible for the creation of these pleasure grounds, but it is likely to have been Adam Ottley (1713-23) who is recorded as spending large sums of money on restoration; his predecessor and successors were largely absent.

Bishop Murray's works were extensive and recorded on a map of 1811. He turned the house around to face east over his newly created parkland with *'properly picturesque'* views, rather than facing west over functional yards. Trees were planted, formal gardens were created to the north of the Palace on the site of the old bowling green/garden, a new lodge built, and a walled kitchen garden was built on the site of the pre-existing unenclosed kitchen garden. Most strikingly a long stone ha-ha was constructed separating the parkland from the great meadow and providing uninterrupted views over the Great Meadow, the Bishop's Pond (a large ox-bow lake formed during a flood of 1802) and up the Tywi valley. This remains one of the most striking elements of the grounds.

Beginning in 1829, Bishop Jenkinson transformed Murray's romantic park into something more in keeping with early/mid-nineteenth century taste. He turned the house back around 180 degrees to face west once again and constructed a new lodge (the current lodge) and drives to serve the new entrance. Sinuous paths were straightened and trees in the parkland and elsewhere removed. The formal gardens to the north of the house were replaced by two circular flowerbeds with a pavilion to the north. A long stone wall was constructed along the northern perimeter of the park and several new outbuildings constructed, including a new home farm just outside the western perimeter of the park. Hot-houses and

View of the pleasure grounds and the Bishop's Palace, 1750 (courtesy of The British Library)

a glass house were erected in the walled garden. These changes are shown on a 1840s estate map in Carmarthenshire Record Office.

During the course of the nineteenth century conifers and deciduous trees as well as rhododendrons and azaleas were planted, so much so that in 1897 Gwenonwy Owen, daughter of Bishop Owen noted the *'huge wonderful chestnut tree … in the centre of the lawn'* the *'enormous cedar tree'* and *'other flowering bushes'*. Three men were at this time employed in the garden, plus *'a man and a woman who spent their time keeping the grounds tidy'*. She also noted that *'exotics such as pineapples and orchids'* were grown in the *'very large and well-cultivated'* kitchen garden. The garden retains some of the fine trees recorded by Gwenonwy Owen.

In 1972 the grounds were divided in two and separated by a concrete fence and by the planting of a line of conifers, with the Church in Wales retaining the western section of the grounds in which they constructed a new Bishop's Palace, and Carmarthenshire County taking over the eastern section including the old Bishop's Palace. A new entrance into the eastern section of the park was established and asphalt-surfaced car parks created inside the entrance. The overall integrity of the park was thus compromised and the relationship between individual elements lost. Since then the visual continuity has been further marred by shrub growth and some unsympathetic planting, and views from the park across the ha-ha have been lost. At the time of writing the Welsh Historic Gardens Trust Carmarthenshire Branch have plans to restore the park and garden to its former glory in partnership with the County Council and the Church in Wales.

The Bishop's Park and Garden is a Grade II Registered Historic Park and Garden.

The Lodge, Bishop's Palace

(photograph: J Holland)

Sources:

British Library. *Prospect from the Palace of Aberguilly* and *East View of the Palace of Aberguilly*, 1750. BL Online Gallery, King George III Topographic Collection, 18 October 2015.

Carmarthenshire Record Office, John Francis Collection, Map of Abergwili Park 1843-58.

Murphy, K. and Ludlow, N., 2004. The Bishop's Park, Abergwili: Historic Landscape Survey, unpublished report by Cambria Archaeology (Dyfed Archaeological Trust).

National Library of Wales, St Davids Map Book, 1796.

National Library of Wales, St Davids Map Book, 1811.

ALBERGWILI PALACE. CARMARTHEN

Old postcard view of The Bishop's Palace taken early 1900s
(courtesy of P Davies)

Broadway

J Holland

No book on historic parks and gardens would be complete without an example of a Messenger glasshouse.

Broadway Hotel, The Peach House (photograph: J Holland)

BROADWAY, Laugharne (SN286097)

No book on historic parks and gardens would be complete without an example of a Messenger glasshouse. One of the great manufacturers of glasshouses in Britain in the nineteenth century was Messenger & Co of Loughborough, horticultural builders, heating engineers and iron founders. Originally manufacturers of iron-work, they branched out into stoves and heating pipes at a time when large country houses were filling their gardens with newly introduced exotics from all over the world. The demand for tender exotics led to a greater understanding of plant requirements for heat, ventilation and light. Messenger & Co met this new demand first by manufacturing heating systems and then designing and producing glasshouses. Their catalogues were illustrated in great detail showing winter gardens and conservatories, verandas, porches, garden shelters, greenhouses, cold frames, pipes and heating stoves; detailing everything required to provide year round growing conditions and protection from the elements. The company closed in 1980, as demand fell, but their records have been retained. They contain amazing details including letters from clients, bills, drawings, even timesheets dating back to the 1800s.

Messenger door handle
(photograph: J Holland)

The archive catalogue of Messenger documents runs to over 200 pages but the only entries for Carmarthenshire are those for stove houses, pipe-work and heating systems at Maesycrugiau and at Derwydd. The lean-to glasshouse at Derwydd has had all its iron-work stripped out, the timber frame has had a basic repair, and the glass has been replaced with corrugated plastic sheet. The glasshouse at Maesycrugiau has gone, only the stone wall around the base and some floor tiles survive. No other examples are recorded in the catalogue.

By chance, looking through some photographs and records taken by a former garden recorder for Pembrokeshire, Gerry Hudson, what looked like a Messenger glasshouse was spotted. Another of his photographs showed a

Broadway Hotel
(photograph: J Holland)

Looking up into the dome
(photograph: J Holland)

door handle plate with the inscription Messenger. On the back was written '*20th June 2000 Broadway*'. Further investigations revealed that the Messenger glasshouse/small conservatory at Broadway is a listed building.

The original house was built in the early seventeenth century for Judge Sir John Powell. It remained in his family until 1802 when the estate was sold to a Mr Watkins of Brecon. By 1810 the house was described as a ruin. In the 1870s a new house was built a little to the west by a Mr Broadwood. It was added to in 1914 and is now a small country hotel and restaurant.

The house consists of two adjoining buildings, the one to the east is single storey, and the other has two storeys with a rounded tower on the western end. Both are fronted with a glazed veranda. The property is on an elevated site south-west of the village of Broadway, overlooking the sea. There is a terrace to the front of the house, with some fine trees. The grounds drop steeply to the road below.

The Messenger conservatory joins the western end of the house via a continuation of the roof to provide a covered access from the house.
It is timber framed with a rubble stone plinth, and small paned glazing. There is a solid wall to the rear. The roof is octagonal, with an unusual ribbed dome, clerestory windows and an iron finial.

When Gerry Hudson visited in 2000 the conservatory was in poor condition and much of the glass was missing. It has since been renovated and re-glazed, and is now called the Peach House.

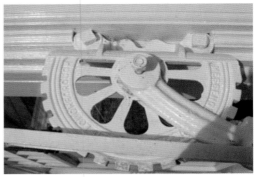

Window opening mechanism, marked Messenger of Loughborough (photograph: J Holland)

Sources:

Photographs from Gerry Hudson.

Jones, F., 1987. *Historic Carmarthenshire Homes and their Families* (Carmarthen: Carmarthenshire Antiquarian Society).

Inside the glasshouse facing towards the house (photograph: J Holland)

Carmarthen Park

K Arblaster

The Park was rich in ornamental iron work presented by local dignitaries, including the octagonal bandstand, two drinking fountains and entrance gates manufactured at Coalbrookdale. The cycle track was Wales' first velodrome and is one of the earliest to survive in working condition.

Carmarthen Park and Cycle Track.

Old postcard from a photograph by J F Lloyd showing the park before its grand opening on Easter Monday 16 April 1900 (courtesy of P Davies)

CARMARTHEN PARK (SN405199)

For some years the people of Carmarthen held sports and cycle races at Llwynywitch fields on the outskirts of the town, north of Picton Terrace. On public holidays people flocked to the town to enjoy the sports and attractions such as hot air balloons and parachutists. By the 1890s, though, the fields were lost to the building boom and Penllwyn Park was built on the site.

By 1896 there were renewed calls for a recreation ground – a People's Park – and a suitable site was identified. Raising money to buy the land from the Ecclesiastical Commissioners and the reversion of the lease from their tenants proved impossible until, in 1899 plans for a park were included in the Carmarthen Improvement Act. This allowed the Corporation to borrow £4000 to acquire and lay out the site. The actual cost was just over £5000 with the shortfall made up by a 1d increase on the rates. The park layout was designed by the Borough Surveyor, Frederick J. Finglah.

When Carmarthen Park opened in 1900 one correspondent to the local newspaper begged that the Corporation *'not let the visitor remark that Carmarthen Park is only a field with seats and a cycle track in it'*. Although there were assurances that shrubs and flowers would soon grow, newspaper articles lamented year after year the lack of flowers and colour throughout the seasons. The Park was however rich in ornamental iron work presented by local dignitaries,

including the octagonal bandstand, two drinking fountains and entrance gates manufactured at Coalbrookdale. The cycle track was Wales' first velodrome and is one of the earliest to survive in working condition. Fred Finglah visited the track at Aston Villa to work out its specifications and was convinced the Carmarthen one would be superior.

Early twentieth century bicycle race at Carmarthen Velodrome (courtesy of Carmarthenshire Museum)

The Park has been used for many events over the years, from agricultural shows and circuses to football matches and concerts. The 1911 National Eisteddfod was held there in a specially constructed wooden pavilion built to hold 12,000 people. Present day events rarely draw that number of people but for over 100 years the Park has met its stated aims of providing somewhere for local youngsters to play, and being a venue for events to attract visitors to the town.

Sources:

Welsh Newspapers Online. *The People's Park at Carmarthen,*1900-04-20, The Carmarthen Weekly Reporter.

Welsh Newspapers Online. *Carmarthen Park,* 1906-04-13, The Carmarthen Weekly Reporter.

Welsh Newspapers Online. *GOOD NEWS FOR CYCLISTS.*1899-04-19, Evening Express.

www.carmarthentowncouncil.gov.uk

Opposite page: Carmarthen Park bandstand (photograph: J Holland)

Court Henry

T Lloyd

Court Henry is one of the ancient houses of the Tywi valley, built in about 1460 by and named after Henry ap Gwilym, of a long established local family and an active commander in Wales during the Wars of the Roses.

COURT HENRY CARMARTHENSHIRE.

The Seat of the Rev.d G.W. Green.

Painting of the house and grounds, note the ornamental cattle in the foreground
(courtesy of T Lloyd)

COURT HENRY, Llangathen (SN556225)

Court Henry is one of the ancient houses of the Tywi valley, built in about 1460 by and named after Henry ap Gwilym, of a long established local family and an active commander in Wales during the Wars of the Roses. Better still, he became father-in-law to the great Sir Rhys ap Thomas KG. The thick walls of his house survive, encased within a re-fronting of the 1730s and a back range added a century later.

The latter was the work of the new purchaser Rev George Wade Green, from London but with Carmarthen cousins, who having increased his modest income by a brilliant marriage to the sister of Sir John Key, later a famous Lord Mayor of London, exchanged a fairly humble higher calling in a small Gloucestershire parish for that of landed gentleman in Wales. Here he proceeded to spend his wife's fortune improving his demesne and doing good Christian works all around. The latter included a new school and a bridge over the river Dulas. His chief work was a brand new estate church with tower, set up on the hill right behind and above the house, as much to be an ornament to his parkland as an acknowledgement of his calling: he took all the services of course. Its peaceable Georgian form has long given way to spiky Victorian gothic and to heavy enlargement, and its park setting is now hard working fields; but its conspicuous siting – a tough climb for old folk - was intended as a highly symbolic parkland monument to the new age of morality.

The house stands at the very foot of this hill, with the public road between church and house sunk down by Green out of sight into a ha-ha. In complete contrast in front lies the broad Tywi valley vista, taking in Nelson's Tower (now generally known as Paxton's Tower) to the south west and looking west to Carmarthen. The river Dulas runs down close beside the house and curves across the front one field below. When Green arrived, the old main road prior to the A40 ran much closer by (only one field before the gates), resulting in an avenue of old oak trees running across three fields long after the road was grassed over in the 1850s, but today less than half a dozen remain.

The immediate grounds of the house were laid out 'de novo', starting at a homely gothic lodge with ornamental gates made by William Moss, the prolific Carmarthen architectural blacksmith. The winding drive meandered down to meet the house at

Court Henry (courtesy of P Davies)

the approved 45 degree angle, nearest to view being an over-elaborate conservatory with a raised drum and dome centre, which lasted only forty years before requiring a simpler rebuild. Demolished in about 1950, it is has just been replaced by a modern version.

In all this, Green was assisted by a friend and neighbour from his Gloucestershire days, Thomas Richardson of Iron Acton, a gentleman with some knowledge of surveying and architecture. He sent Green three watercolour designs for the lodge, in the spirit of John Nash's cottages at Blaise Castle near Bristol, plus instructions on how to set the iron railed fence to divide the front lawn from the park beyond. This latter survives: the lodge designs were all too large and a simpler one, though in the same ornamental spirit, was chosen.

Not much obviously survives now from Green's planting. Several oaks look old enough. The best is a remarkably tall and handsome yew tree, split three ways from the base, one arm of which sadly fell in Spring 2015, but still remains rooted and rests securely propped on its branches at a 45 degree angle. A mighty copper beech (its dead top surgically removed) behind the house shows only as a sapling in a photo of about 1880. A big white quartz boulder circular rockery proved too much trouble in the 1960s, but another survives with a yew tree on top and a pathway between giving access via an archway from garden to back drive. A great horse-chestnut, whose lower branches had touched the ground and sprouted up to create a perfect dome, fell apart in a great storm in the 1970s. Rhododendrons thrive as ever all too well, but the days of the ponticums might soon be numbered. Post-war plantings include a dawn redwood and a ginko, both growing at huge speed.

The new estate church built as much as a garden feature as an acknowledgement to his calling (photograph: J Holland)

Derwydd Mansion

J Holland

Derwydd garden is included in Cadw's *Register of Landscapes, Parks and Gardens of Special Historical Interest in Wales* and described as 'a small late nineteenth-century garden with surviving iron work, topiary, walled garden, walks, croquet lawn, incorporating earlier features including a pre-1809 terrace'.

Aerial photograph. The walled garden clearly visible, is dived into four quadrants
(courtesy Dr J D Davies)

DERWYDD, Llandybie (SN612178)

Derwydd Mansion is tucked into the south-facing slope of a valley formed by the Afon Marlais. It lies to the west of the hamlet of Derwydd, and between Llandeilo and Ammanford. Derwydd garden is included in Cadw's *Register of Landscapes, Parks and Gardens of Special Historical Interest in Wales* and described as: 'a small late nineteenth-century garden with surviving iron work, topiary, walled garden, walks, croquet lawn, incorporating earlier features including a pre-1809 terrace'. The house is listed Grade II*:

Photograph of Derwydd 1948
(courtesy of Dr J D Davies)

The listing suggests that the earliest part of the house was fifteenth-century, perhaps older. The first reference is to Hywel ap Bebo and his wife who were recorded there in 1550. Their great, great grand-daughter Sage married into the Vaughan Family of Golden Grove; their descendant Elizabeth married Sir Thomas Stepney of Llanelli, whose daughter married Joseph Gulston in 1767. The property, through the marriages of six heiresses, remained in the same family until the last of the Stepney Gulstons, Joy, moved into Llandeilo and sold the estate in 1999. It was sold again in 2013 to the current owners.

The contents were sold in September 1998 by Sotheby's while the estate was divided into 14 lots and sold the following year. The estate at that time included 240 acres of land, the mansion house with estate cottages, farm and woodlands. At the subsequent sale in 2013 the mansion house was sold with 8 acres.

The fifteenth-century range, aligned north-south, had two wings on the west side nearest the road. In 1670 it had 18 hearths. Part of the house may have been demolished in the 1820s but it wasn't until the 1880s that Alan Stepney Gulston added substantially to the house, using local architect David Jenkins. The extension was built into the slope, on the terraces to the north of the house. Internally the extension is stepped on the terraces, on the same level as the first floor of the older Tudor mansion.

Fenton, in his *Tours of Wales*, described Derwydd in 1809 as '*an irregular building. Had a large court before it, and Gardens behind it, on a declivity with terraces. Enter the Garden from a landing place of stairs.*' The 1880s addition created a multi-gabled building, with a rough cast screed and mullioned windows. It has stone roofs and brick chimneys. At the back of the house is a long wooden conservatory. Part of the conservatory roof is glazed whilst the remainder is of corrugated iron. Photographs indicate that the conservatory may have been L-shaped.

The house is approached through a new iron gate, hung between substantial stone piers in an opening in the wall, which surrounds the property on three sides. The carriage drive marked on the First Edition 1:2500 Ordnance Survey map is shown running in a diagonal line from west to south-east to the stables and outbuildings. Fenton refers to a large court before the house. The Second Edition map shows the drive branching, one branch to the north-east and the side of the nineteenth-century extension, the other south-east to the front of the house. Today some large trees have been felled to the east of the drive, but a number of tall conifers remain. To the right of the lower section of the drive, amongst the trees, is a small building.

DERWYDD, NR. LLANDILO.

Old Postcard of Derwydd (courtesy of P Davies)

The garden and pleasure grounds comprise a number of distinct areas: the planting around the house, the walled garden, the orchard, the woodland walks and painting lawn, the terraces and the croquet lawn. Much of the original terracing was lost when the house was enlarged.

Photographs of the family, taken in the early 1900s, show exotic planting around the house. One shows a line

Derwydd Italian garden in the foreground and conservatory, 1948 (courtesy of Dr J D Davies)

of *Phormium tenax* on the upper terrace. Another shows Alan Stepney Gulston standing next to a *Trachycarpus fortunei*. The ground rises steeply around the house. To the east of the house is the croquet lawn. Above this, one of the terraces is now topped with overgrown rhododendrons, cherry laurel, and azaleas. There is evidence at the base of the terrace of a rill and kidney shaped pond, which were recorded in the Cadw register, but have yet to be restored. A recent addition is a willow tunnel to the east of the house. The original flower borders around the house have been lost, together with much of the topiary.

To the north and back of the house, under the main windows, are stone steps leading up to a narrow grassed terrace. There is a further flight of steps leading from the terrace up to the walled garden. The walled garden is some 3 metres higher than the back of the house and is faced on the south side by a retaining wall, and accessed via the steps. The garden is walled on three sides with the wall on the fourth side being below the walled garden, in front of the house, forming a retaining wall to the garden and terrace. The front or fourth side is therefore open. The garden is almost level with the roof. The walls may have existed prior to Fenton's visit in 1809; they appear on the 1840 tithe map. The summerhouse was added by 1887.

The north wall is divided in the centre by a stone two-storeyed summerhouse, which has a pyramidal tiled roof with a weather vane on the top. The summerhouse has a fireplace on the ground floor, with a brick built surround, constructed using hand-made bricks, which are irregular in size. It has a blocked-up doorway on both sides, and a fine oak staircase rising to the floor above. On the first floor is a store which has been lined with shelves.

To the west of the summerhouse is a lean-to glasshouse, which was commissioned by Alan Stepney Gulston in 1894. In a series of letters to Messenger & Co of Loughborough, he sets out his requirements for a plant house and stove house to be constructed by them (see attached letters). The pipework for the heating system was still evident in the 1990s but has since been lost. The lean-tos no longer have their original glass or timber. The red tiled floor, gratings and underfloor reservoirs survive. The grapevine still bears fruit and a mature peach tree survives.

Behind the north-facing wall and glasshouse, adjoining the summerhouse, is the boundary wall which runs parallel with the north wall of the walled garden. The outline of what were the potting sheds can be seen against this wall. The covers from now absent cold-frames lean against the wall. A cold-frame can be seen in front of the summerhouse in one of the early photos, with Agnes Gulston. They bear a plaque which reads 'Halliday, Middleton, Manchester.' There is a curved structure in the back of the wall, which may relate to the heating system for the glasshouse, and a sunken area in the grass which may have been the pit for the stove, or cistern. Alan Stepney Gulston's letters refer to a coal chute. All the iron-work has been removed.

On the eastern wall, facing west, are a number of overgrown fruit trees which would have been trained against the wall. The walled garden has two openings, one on the west wall which is wide enough to accommodate a cart, and a pedestrian entrance on the east side. Both entrances are lined with dressed stone, in contrast to the rubble stone built walls. The west entrance is arched above the wall. The iron fixings for the gates remain, but the gates have been removed for restoration.

There is a sundial in the centre of the walled garden, which was erected in 1900. The brass top-plate is mounted on a vase-shaped pedestal. Early photographs show the garden divided into four cultivated quadrants, but today the entire enclosure has been grassed over. A few old espaliered trees remain.

The Cadw register records a series of iron hoops, which led from the top of the steps into the walled garden and are depicted in family photographs carrying roses. The only remaining ironwork in the walled garden is a structure, with a central hoop with hoops at right angles on both sides, which may have carried hops. This has been restored and is located by the eastern pedestrian entrance.

The eastern gateway leads through woodland to what was described as the 'painting' lawn, which is now a rough open area, among brambles. It has extensive views towards the Black Mountains, with Carreg Cennen castle clearly visible to the west. The family enjoyed painting the view from here. In the woodland are a series of *gorsedd* stones, placed there prior to 1906.

The western entrance leads to another enclosure running north south on sloping ground, and may have been an orchard. This runs down to the west of the house. The pond to the south of the house and grounds has gone.

The house and grounds are being restored by their current owners. They are not open to the public.

Derwydd is a Grade II Registered Historic Park and Garden.

Sources:

British Newspaper Archive.

Cadw: Welsh Historic Monuments, 2002. *Register of Landscapes, Parks and Gardens of Special Historic Interest in Wales. Part 1: Parks and Gardens* (Cardiff: Cadw).

Fisher, J. (ed.), 1917. *Tours in Wales (1804-1813) by Richard Fenton* (London: Cambrian Archaeological Association).

Derwydd walled garden and summer house, 1948
(courtesy Dr J D Davies)

Jones, F., 1987. *Historic Carmarthenshire Homes and their Families* (Carmarthen: Carmarthenshire Antiquarian Society).

Lloyd, T., Orbach, J. and Scourfield, R., 2006. *The Buildings of Wales: Carmarthenshire and Ceredigion* (New Haven: Yale University Press).

Museum of English Rural Life, letters, plans, and invoices from the Messenger papers.

National Library of Wales, photographic collections.

Notes taken during meeting with R Dallavalle October 2015.

Ordnance Survey 1:2500 First and Second Edition maps, 1878, 1906.

Restoration of the gardens 2015
(photograph: J Holland)

The summerhouse and remains of a
Messenger lean-to glasshouse 2015
(photograph: J Holland)

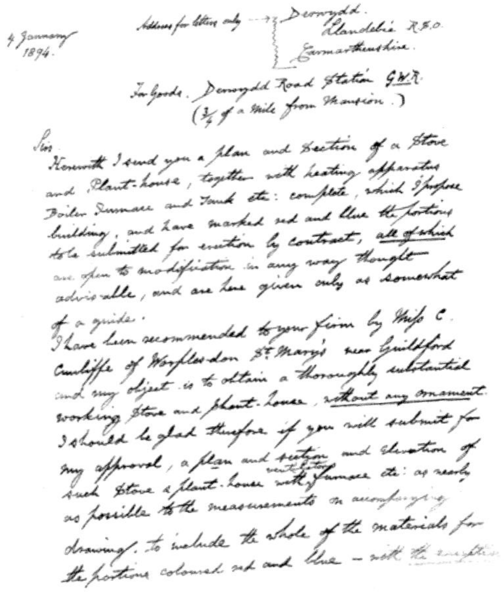

4 January 1894   Address for letters only   Derwydd

Llandebie. RSO

Carmarthenshire

For Goods Derwydd Road Station GWR

(3/4 mile from Mansion)

Sirs

Herewith I send you a plan and section of a Stove and Plant-house, together with heating apparatus Boiler Furnace and Tank etc. complete, which I Propose building, and have marked red and blue the portions to be submitted for erection by contract, <u>all of which</u> are open to modification in any way thought advisable, and here given only as somewhat of a guide.

I have been recommended to your firm by Philip C Canliffe of Worplesdon St Mary's near Guildford, and my object is to obtain a thoroughly substantial working stove and plant-house, without any ornament.

I should be glad therefore if you will submit for my approval, a plan and section and elevation of such stove & plant-house with ventilators, furnace etc. as nearly as possible to the measurements on accompanying drawing, to include the whole of the materials for the portions coloured red and blue- with the exception of the red bricks, fire bricks drainpipes (tile) and the haulage from station and labour.

I should require you to send a thoroughly competent man to supervise the erection of the whole complete work together with a competent bricklayer. Kindly let your price for above, cover all outlay as above, also specify time.

You will observe that the chimney stack would be of brick carried up against and partly within wall, and would include flue for grate in Tool & Potting shed, in addition to furnace flue.

The two chimney-pots to be of same colour as the outside red-brick-work.

All water from Glass roof to be conducted into Tank which should be fitted with an overflow as well as Service Tap and an emptying tap into drain.

I should not require inside staging

I am

Sirs

Yours very truly

Alan Stepney-Gulston

Letter reproduced courtesy Museum of English Rural Life.

Dinefwr Park

K Murphy

Dinefwr Park is noted for its late eighteenth/early
nineteenth-century landscape park of rolling grassland, tree
clumps and woodland. It also includes highly important
earlier elements, including the medieval Dinefwr Castle.

*Aquatint by James Bretherton of about 1790 showing the Dinefwr landscape following the removal of
the formal gardens*

DINEFWR PARK, Llandeilo (SN 614225)

Dinefwr Park is noted for its late eighteenth/early nineteenth-century landscape park of rolling grassland, tree clumps and woodland. It also includes highly important earlier elements, including the medieval Dinefwr Castle which was transformed in the seventeenth century into a summerhouse/banqueting hall and eye-catcher; a deer park, veteran oak trees, picturesque walks, remnants of avenues, and later elements such as the ha-ha around the house and an ice-house.

Dinefwr Park is one of the most complex and best documented historic landscapes in Wales. Where else can one find an Iron Age fort, not one but two Roman forts, not one but two deserted medieval towns, a medieval castle, a major house, a seventeenth-century park and a celebrated late eighteenth/early nineteenth-century parkland landscape? Space here only allows for a brief historical summary; much more comprehensive accounts can be found in the sources below.

Rhys ap Gruffydd chose a hill overlooking the Tywi valley to build one of his chief castles in 1163. Originally of timber, the castle was rebuilt in stone; much of what remains dates to the thirteenth and fourteenth centuries. A settlement developed outside the castle gates, which later grew into a small town. Edward I, following his conquest of Wales in the late thirteenth century, founded a new town some distance from the castle on lower-lying ground. For several centuries the two towns ran in parallel, divided along racial lines, the Welsh 'Upper Town' or 'Old Town' around the castle and English 'New Town', both slowly declining and largely deserted by the end of the medieval period. In 1532, John Leland described the New Town, or Newton as it was then known, as '*sumtime a long streat nowe ruinus*'. Fields would have surrounded the towns, traces of which can still be detected in the landscape.

Newton House in about 1967 (courtesy Carmarthenshire Museum)

In the late medieval period, the long association of Dinefwr with the Rhys (Rice) family continued with Sir Rhys ap Thomas (died 1525). His substantial eight-bedroom Newton House, lay within the ruinous town.

There are no records of gardens or a park connected with the medieval Dinefwr

Newton House from the East
(courtesy of National Trust)

Castle nor with Rhys ap Thomas's house, but he was noted as a man with '*a passion for parks and hunting*', and it may be that the deer park at Abermarlais, one of Rhys's other properties in the Tywi valley, twelve kilometres from Dinefwr, provided sufficient opportunities for the chase. Alternatively, it may be that the absence of a deer park associated with the medieval castle and Newton House was due to ample land (and game) available for the chase within a short ride.

During the sixteenth and early seventeenth centuries the Rhys family, or Rice as they were by then known, continued to add to their Dinefwr/Newton estate, with the first clear evidence of a park and garden emerging under the guidance of Edward and Walter Rice from 1659, and then after the death of Edward in 1663, by Walter and his wife Dorothy. They replaced old Newton House with a three-storey, double-pile house (which survives beneath nineteenth-century stone cladding), created a deer park and laid out gardens. In order to carry out these improvements one of the first things they had to do was realign the main public road down the Tywi valley that ran from Llandeilo to the east, through what had been the town of Newton, and on to Carmarthen in the west. It was moved to the

north, immediately outside the soon to be created stone-wall boundary of their deer park. The deer park lay to the west of Newton House. Sections of its boundary survive to full height, including the wall alongside the realigned public road mentioned above and the wall forming the western and south-eastern limits of the park. Some sections are ruinous, such as those running along the valley bottom to the south-west of house, and others have disappeared, including the eastern boundary that must have run north-south to the west of the

Newton House from the North
These two paintings hang in Newton House and show the formal gardens and landscape as it was in about 1700
(courtesy of National Trust)

house. In total just over 40 hectares (100 acres) were enclosed. One of the most striking elements of the deer park is the large number of veteran oak trees within its compass, most of which must have been several centuries old in the mid seventeenth century. Careful examination of these shows that they sit on the levelled boundaries of the medieval field system of the town of Newton, or that they lie alongside the old, realigned road that ran through the park. Formal

Old postcard showing an aerial view of Newton House

gardens were laid out to the north and west of the house. These are shown on two oil paintings dating to about 1700 that currently hang in Newton House.

The perspectives of the paintings are difficult to reconcile with each other and with the landscape as it is now, but it is clear that the gardens comprised rectangular parterres separated by formal paths and geometrically planted shrubs enclosed by walls, hedges and fences characteristic of the late seventeenth century. Some writers have expressed doubts about whether these gardens existed in the form shown in the paintings, but a geophysical survey followed by archaeological excavations revealed their remains immediately below the turf to the west of the house.

Old postcard showing a view of Dinefwr Castle. These two postcards are taken from an aerial survey shortly after World War II . The first shows the site of Nissen huts used during the war (courtesy of P Davies)

Outside the formal gardens and park grounds the home farm was established to the south of the house, with a walled garden, presumably functioning as a kitchen garden, a little further away. The barns and other outbuildings of the farm have been incorporated into the inner and outer courtyards attached to Newton House and now serve as offices and private dwellings. New grounds were also laid out to the east, north and south of the house, including several avenues of trees. Most of the trees from these avenues were removed in the latter part of the eighteenth century, but a few still survive, including Spanish chestnut around the current carpark, and a line of limes. One of the avenues ran from the house to the south up to Castle Woods, bringing the woods and the area around the castle into the ornamental parkland. Clumps of trees were also planted in this period – these are shown on the paintings noted above. Not only did the Castle form a distinctive eye-catcher, but an upper storey capped with a conical roof was added to the great round tower to serve as a summerhouse and banqueting room. A cold bath house within the deer park probably also dates to this period; it may be the small building depicted in the background of an oil painting hanging in Newton House. Many of these elements formed the core of the late eighteenth-century park described below.

The Rices continued to add more land to the Dinefwr estate throughout the early and mid-eighteenth century and undertook improvements to the house, park and gardens, such as moving the home farm from Newton House to its present location 650m to the north-east. However, it was not until after the marriage of George Rice, the then owner of Dinefwr, to Cecil Talbot in 1756 that major changes were made. It would seem that Cecil was the inspiration and driving force behind these changes for by 1757 improvements are recorded. Most of the work was to the east of the house, transforming farmland into rolling parkland. Hedges were removed, trees grubbed up and scrub cleared. Some of the trees in the avenues were chopped down and trees planted around the survivors to form clumps; new tree clumps were also planted. A new drive was constructed and the whole of the eastern portion of the estate emparked, bringing the medieval Llandyfeisant Church into the compass of the park as an eye-catcher.

In 1775, George Rice invited Lancelot 'Capability' Brown to visit Dinefwr and provide advice. By then Cecil and George Rice had completed their work and so it is probable that they were seeking professional approbation for their work rather than requesting an overall design. Nevertheless, Brown made several recommendations for improvement, some of which were acted on.

This interesting postcard shows the former thatched lodge, now replaced by a stone-built tudor-gothic building. The veteran oak was clearly much prized – its stump can still be seen just inside the gates to the park (courtesy of P Davies)

For instance, the kitchen garden was relocated from close to the house to the home farm, some planting was undertaken, a new drive was built (the current main drive into the estate), and a walk in the picturesque style laid out. This walk, known as the Brownian Walk or the Precipice Walk where it runs along the steep valley side below the castle, runs from Newton House through The

Old postcard of Dinefwr, front of the house
(courtesy P Davies)

Rookery. Here views of the house, the castle and down the Tywi valley are glimpsed through the woods, on to the castle, and then along the valley side returning to the house across the parkland. Other shorter picturesque walks with small rustic stone bridges in the deer park may also be the result of Brown's advice.

By the late eighteenth century all the major elements of the park had been completed. Over the following 220 years embellishments (and disfigurements) were generally minor. However, one of the more significant changes occurred to Newton House. In the 1850s, the lawns that swept up to the house were interrupted by the construction of a cumbersome ha-ha within which lay flower gardens, and the exterior of the house was transformed into a gothic mansion by the addition of stone cladding. Later a billiard room was added to the south side of the house in the same gothic style, and later still a tennis court (now gone) was constructed to the north of the ha-ha. New lodges and other buildings were added in the later nineteenth century, the red-brick construction of some of them contrasting with the older stone buildings. Wellingtonias planted in the late nineteenth century are now striking elements of the park. In 1907, Lord Dynevor donated the eastern tip of the park to the people of Llandeilo as a public park (Park Penlan). This has been municipalised with tarmac paths and a bandstand, and separated from Dinefwr Park by iron railings. The north-east corner of the park is now occupied by Llandeilo rugby ground, Cae William. During the mid and late twentieth century the Dynevors sold off some buildings and parts of the park. The eastern part of the park was given over to agriculture and much of its parkland character was lost. Newton House and much of the park are now owned by the National Trust, which since the early 2000s has been undertaking a programme of landscape restoration, including changing arable land back to meadow. Some elements of the park, such as the rugby ground, are irretrievably changed, but most retain the character of a late eighteenth-century parkland landscape with a wealth of earlier features.

Dinefwr Park is open to the public - Newton House and the park are owned by the National Trust. Castle Woods and Dinefwr Castle are owned by the Wildlife Trust of South and West Wales.

Dinefwr is a Grade I Registered Historic Park and Garden.

Sources:

Cadw: Welsh Historic Monuments, 2002. *Register of Landscapes, Parks and Gardens of Special Historic Interest in Wales. Part 1: Parks and Gardens* (Cardiff: Cadw).

Colvin and Moggridge, 2003. Parc Dinefwr: designed landscape survey, unpublished report for the National Trust.

Morgan, G., 2014. *Dinefwr: A Phoenix in Wales* (Llandysul: Gomer).

Schlee, D., 2008. Excavation and Survey at Dinefwr Park, Llandeilo, Carmarthenshire, unpublished report by Dyfed Archaeological Trust.

Old postcard of Dinefwr c.1900s, back of the house (courtesy P Davies)

Dolaucothi

K Arblaster

All that remains of the old house today is part of one wing, used as a farmhouse. The remains of the park and garden are in the wide flood plain of the river – Dolaucothi means 'meadows of the Cothi'

Old photograph of the house (courtesy of P Davies)

DOLAUCOTHI, Cynwyl Gaeo (SN665408)

The Dolaucothi Estate around the village of Pumpsaint came into the ownership of the Johnes family of Abermarlais in the 1500s. It continued in the male line of the same family, and in the eighteenth century became linked by marriage to the Knights of Croft Castle and to Thomas Johnes of Hafod. John Nash made some additions to the house in the 1790s and it was extended again in the 1870s. Following WWII, when it had been requisitioned by the Ministry of Supply, its condition was so poor that it was largely demolished in the 1950s. All that remains of the old house today is part of one wing, used as a farmhouse.

The remains of the park and garden are in the wide flood plain of the river – Dolaucothi means *'meadows of the Cothi'*. There are two drives which led to the house; the first, leading off the main road through the village flanked by a lodge house, was explored by George Borrow. He described an avenue of *'very noble oaks'* alongside a *'beautiful brook'* and thought he had never seen *'a more pleasing locality'*.

Today the walk is still lovely, especially in spring when the bluebells are in flower, but the old oaks are gone, their stumps hidden among the beech trees that line the drive today.

At the point where the path from the north drive enters the old parkland there is a gnarled sycamore known for some reason as 'Old Lumpy'. Thought to be perhaps 300 years old this could be the oldest tree on the estate. Just in front of this, another sycamore throws a root over a stone structure, possibly a dipping well.

Dolaucothi House (courtesy of The National Library of Wales)

The second drive, built to the south in the 1830s, crosses the Cothi on a wooden bridge known as the Ogofau Bridge. Ogofau means caves, a reference to the nearby goldmine workings which are part of the estate. This route leads back along the far side of the river through plantings of Irish yew, Atlas cedar, Austrian pine, Algerian fir and two forms of Lawson's cypress. Diary entries for 1834 and 1835 headed *'Remarks on the Season'* by an unknown writer mention American shrubs, *hedera canadensis* and *mesphilus canadensis*, suggesting that there were keen gardeners in the family at that time. Letters in the Dolaucothi Collection at the National

Dolaucothi avenue (photograph: J James)

Library of Wales refer to a mature lime avenue being destroyed by gales in 1836-37. Some stumps remain which might be evidence of this avenue, but the four large limes standing in the park today are younger, possibly planted after the gales. The park is separated from the lawn of the house by a stone ha-ha. The most modern walled garden stands to the south east, the walls at their highest stand about 3m tall but are crumbling in places. A map from the 1770s shows two enclosed gardens to the west of the house; these had disappeared by the time of the Tithe map in 1840. Outside the south-east corner of the walls there are the remains of a flower garden, probably once lined by the box shrubs still growing there. Lumps and chippings of quartz are also prevalent in this area, suggesting a path dressed and edged with the material. There are some fine specimen trees in this area too, including Norway spruce and Douglas fir.

The descendants of the Johnes family gifted Dolaucothi to the National Trust in the 1950s and today there is a way-marked circular walk around the two drives, as well as longer walks up into the woods and hills which surround the parkland.

Dolaucothi is a Grade II Registered Historic Park and Garden.

Sources:

Borrow, G., 1862. *Wild Wales*. Project Gutenberg, 14 October 2015.

Cadw: Welsh Historic Monuments, 2002. *Register of Landscapes, Parks and Gardens of Special Historic Interest in Wales. Part 1: Parks and Gardens* (Cardiff: Cadw).

Edwinsford

K Arblaster

Edwinsford is set in a beautiful position in the Cothi valley where the river meanders towards the Towy to the south-west.

Edwinsford House (courtesy of Talley History Society)

EDWINSFORD, Llansawel (SN631345)

Edwinsford is set in a beautiful position in the Cothi valley where the river meanders towards the Tywi to the south-west. The oldest part of the house dates from about 1635, with major additions made in the early 1700s and the mid 1860s. A wooded hillside to the south forms a picturesque backdrop to the house, as it did in the 1770s when Paul Sandby recorded it in a lithograph.

By the time of the tithe return in 1838 the estate was owned by Sir James Williams; the last member of this Williams Drummond family died in 1970. The Edwinsford estate had been sold off long before that, with most of the surrounding farms sold in 1919 and the house and grounds reputedly willed to the family butler. The estate buildings across the river, once identified by intricate lead figures showing their function, are now private houses.

The tithe map shows a carriage drive circling Moelfre hill. Following the remodelling of the house in the 1860s a new entrance drive was created, leading from Iron Gate Lodge which was built on the Talley road in 1861. This entrance is flanked by 2m high stone pillars and dressed-stone walls topped with iron railings. The drive is still lined with rhododendrons. There were two other lodges, one at the top of an oak lined lane. These oaks, few of which remain, were identified as *Quercus robur*, the English oak and not *Quercus petraea* which is a native to Wales, suggesting they were planted deliberately.

Richard Fenton visited Edwinsford in the early 1800s and described '*a large walled garden, a great part of which is mud, said to be the best for fruit*'. The area enclosed is about 6.5 acres; today a few pear trees, some very overgrown box hedging and the remnants of a glasshouse and dividing gateways are all that remain. The walled garden is adjacent to Gardener's Cottage, the grandest of the

Aquatint of Edwinsford by Paul Sandby, 1776
(courtesy of Carmarthenshire Museum)

group of estate buildings on the far side of the bridge. This is a single span structure which replaced that shown in Sandby's image. It was designed by the Edwards brothers, sons of the architect of the famous bridge at Pontypridd. It incorporates a moulded stone which Tom Lloyd suggests is the base of a fine sundial, made by the royal clockmaker in about 1710, which once stood in the gardens. The brass upper part of this is now in Carmarthen Museum. Another sundial, a 1.5m tall sandstone obelisk, was moved after 1954 from its position in front of the house to its current home outside one of the cottages.

Photographs taken in 1871 show a formal circular lawn in front of the house, rhododendron and possibly gunnera along the riverside walk, and neatly trimmed box hedges. By 1954 the gardens and pleasure grounds were becoming overgrown; today the current owners have had to prioritise clearing the area to get encroaching water away in an attempt to save the remains of the house.

There is no public access to Edwinsford nor its estate cottages, which are largely hidden behind a high stone wall, but there are lovely views from the oak-lined lane to the north of Talley lakes. The house is in a very poor condition and probably beyond saving.

Edwinsford is a Grade II Registered Historic Park and Garden.

A recent photograph of Edwinsford (courtesy of Talley History Society)

Sources:

Cadw: Welsh Historic Monuments, 2002. *Register of Landscapes, Parks and Gardens of Special Historic Interest in Wales. Part 1: Parks and Gardens* (Cardiff: Cadw).

Lloyd, T., 1986. *The Lost Houses of Wales* (London: Save Britain's Heritage).

www.Coflein.gov.uk

Images of leaden figures formerly at Edwinsford: 'The Boar'; 'Mercury with Caduceus' and 'The Gamekeeper' from sketches by Pte. Joseph Milner 7th Batt. Manchester Regiment (courtesy of Carmarthenshire Record Office)

Garden of Eden
(Glyn Aur)

J Holland

Glyn Aur was once famous for its cottage garden of elaborate topiary, depicting biblical scenes.

Old postcard of the Garden of Eden (courtesy P Davies)

THE GARDEN OF EDEN – GLYN AUR, Abergwili (SN436221)

Glyn Aur was once famous for its cottage garden of elaborate topiary, depicting biblical scenes. Situated to the north of the village of Abergwili on the Castell Pigyn Road, it was created in the early 1900s by a Mr D Davies. The garden surrounded a small Victorian house, with a long veranda-style porch at the front and a lean-to greenhouse to the side. The clipped topiary represented scenes of the Last Supper, the Flight into Egypt, the Crucifixion, Herod's Feast, the Garden of Eden and the Guardian Angel.

Mr Davies was not only a keen gardener, but was also a photographer, and is remembered for the series of postcards he had printed of his garden. He opened his garden to the public, and charged 6d a visit. The postcards were in print until the 1940s, and are sold and collected today.

The garden did not survive beyond his death, and the house has since been demolished.

*Old postcards of the
Garden of Eden
(courtesy of P Davies)*

Gellideg

J Holland

Gellideg has one of the finest collections in
Carmarthenshire of rhododendrons, azaleas,
camellias and magnolias. It is very much a
plantsman's garden with many unusual trees
and shrubs.

Gellideg, 1830
(courtesy of E Atkinson)

GELLIDEG, Llandyfaelog (SN422105)

Gellideg has one of the finest collections in Carmarthenshire of rhododendrons, azaleas, camellias and magnolias. It is very much a plantsman's garden with many unusual trees and shrubs.

As with many country estates that span several hundred years, the site has developed to meet the needs of each generation. The house underwent many additions before it became redundant in 1946; it became a ruin, and was replaced by a modern and fairly modest house in the 1960s. Development can be divided into four main periods:

1820 Late Georgian parkland when the drives were laid out, the lodge was built together with the ha-ha, walled garden, belvedere, stables, ponds and parkland;

1851 A Victorian Italianate addition to the house of a conservatory, a Campanile tower, terracing and Victorian flower beds;

1966-98 The new house and planting by Margaret Jennings and Trevor Crosby, and the current period of restoration by Edwin and Mary Atkinson.

The history of the site goes back to the 1560s when Gellideg was a tenanted farmhouse. By the 1700s the farm consisted of 98 acres and was part of the estate of the Lloyds of Alltycadno in Llangynderyn. It was one of the properties settled on Maria Elizabeth Catherine Lloyd who married William Clayton in 1761. Their son sold Gellideg to Sir William Clayton in 1811 for £1200.

It was sold again in 1820 to Richard Thomas Dixie.

Richard Thomas Dixie incorporated the farmhouse into a small two storey Georgian country residence. The old farmhouse was

The mansion ruin (photograph: J Holland)

converted into a service wing. Richard was also responsible for the lodge, walled garden, stable block and courtyard, the belvedere and drives. The belvedere was built a short distance from the house at the south-western end of the walled garden, with commanding views over the Gwendraeth valley, across Carmarthen Bay to the distant hills of the Gower peninsula.

Dixie emigrated to Canada in 1834 where he died. Having been unsuccessful in selling the property before he left, it was sold in 1839 by his executors to Major General Sir James

Gellideg before the Italianate addition of 1851 (courtesy of E Atkinson)

Cockburn (Paymaster and Inspector General of Royal Marines). It was sold again to Richard Jennings in 1849 and has remained in the Jennings family to this day.

Richard Jennings commissioned the Carmarthen architect William Wesley Jenkins to build a larger mansion around the original house. This was built with an Italianate tower in the Campanile style. The design for the house was influenced by the fashion popularised by John Nash, who designed Osborne House on the Isle of Wight for Prince Albert in 1845.

In 1852 the first conservatory was added to the house. This was constructed of steel and glass with a curved roof, influenced perhaps by the design of the Crystal Palace by Joseph Paxton in 1851. It is thought to have been constructed by Fox and Henderson of

Birmingham, who built the Crystal Palace. Fox and Henderson specialised in railway equipment and were responsible for the construction of the roofs of the Liverpool Street Station, Paddington and Birmingham New Street Station. The company went into administration in 1856 and broke up a year later. Construction of the conservatory in 1852 fits the time period in which they were active.

Gellideg 1852 prior to the extension. With its first conservatory
(courtesy E Atkinson)

The mansion was extended again between 1880 and 1927 adding a billiard room, bedrooms and a new conservatory. The new conservatory was a more elaborate affair. Richard Jennings died in 1891 and his son Richard Edward Jennings inherited the property. He died in 1908 and Gellideg passed to his eldest son, Lt Col Edwards Charles Jennings CBE. He added the farmhouse and cart shed which was built near the stables. Following the end of the Second World War Lt Col Edward Jennings moved out of the mansion to live in Brighton.

In 1946 the house was no longer required, the lead was removed from the roof, and the mansion fell into disrepair and became a ruin. Lt Col Edward Jennings died in 1953 and the property passed to his son Lt Col Christopher Jennings DL MBE. In 1961-2 he built a new house incorporating the belvedere at the west end of the walled garden. This has stunning views across Carmarthen Bay.

From the mid 1960s Margaret Jennings took on the garden with the help of Trevor Crosby, retired former Curator of the Leeds University Botanic Gardens. Much of the rich and varied planting from this

House showing the second conservatory
(courtesy E Atkinson)

period has survived. The gardens contain many rhododendron species including *R. Arboreum; R. Augustinii; R. Bureavii; R. Campanulatum; R. Falconeri; R. Maddenii; R. Sino Falconeri; R. Thomsonii; R. Williamsianum*: and *R. Yunnanense.* Magnolias include *M. Sieboldii; M. Stellata* and *M. Wilsonii.*

There are many other interesting plants, including azaleas, roses and hydrangeas. Particularly of note *are Embothrium coccineum, Crinondendron hookerianum, Skimmia × media Kew Green, Enkianthus campanulatus,* and *Prunus padus Wateri.*

The gardens are made up of the walled garden, the old garden around the ruined mansion and the Cottage Garden developed by Trevor Crosby.

The walled garden is divided into four quadrants with traditional cross-paths and a central dipping pond. In the 1960s a small swimming pool was added, which has been converted into an ornamental lily pool. This is now an ornamental garden, with lawns and flowerbeds. It has a line of rose arches that runs north-south. There are the remains of two lean-to glasshouses against the north wall. Substantial heating pipes remain which would indicate that the glasshouses were heated by a hot water system. Against the west wall are a number of unusual trees including a *Staphylea colchica* and a *Parrotia persica.*

There was a Victorian garden around the mansion, which no longer exists. The remains of the ornamental balustrading survive at one end of the house. The conservatory has gone, but a mature *Pittosporum tennuifolium* still stands against the house. As a native of New Zealand these are often tender, but the ruined walls of the mansion have provided sufficient shelter for it to thrive. The remains of the conservatory are still visible on the ground, with paving, and a low stone wall. Below ground level, behind the conservatory the heating system can be seen, with a stove and header tank surviving.

Victorian flower beds and balustrade
(courtesy E Atkinson)

The cottage garden is to the east of the new house and contains many duplicates of the shrubs and plants from the other gardens.

Beside the cart shed is a large pool with a slope going down into the water, which would have been used for washing carts. Its perimeter has been planted with conifers. The old mansion is hidden by trees. The ha-ha runs from the northern entry to the property, around the perimeter of the gardens to the old mansion, and ends at the belvedere. It is over 200 metres long, but only a few feet high. It was topped by park railings, to keep out grazing cattle and sheep. There are substantial trees in the parkland which drops steeply away from the house. Gellideg is a beautiful mature garden filled with interesting specimens. It is not open to the public, but the current residents Edwin and Mary Atkinson generously open the garden to organised groups. They are restoring the gardens and have catalogued many of the trees and shrubs.

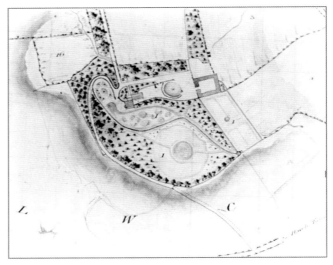

Estate Map of Gellideg 1830
(courtesy: E Atkinson)

Sources:

Atkinson, Edwin. Notes compiled on Gellideg.

Jones, F., 1987. *Historic Carmarthenshire Homes and their Families* (Carmarthen: Carmarthenshire Antiquarian Society).

Lloyd, T., 1986. *The Lost Houses of Wales* (London: Save Britain's Heritage).

www.parksandgardens.org

An old swimming pool finds a new use as an ornamental lily pool, Gellideg (photograph: J Holland)

Glynhir

K Murphy

Glynhir comprises a small landscape park with associated walled kitchen-garden, dovecote, icehouse, water-management features and picturesque woodland walks dating to the early, mid and late nineteenth century. The water-management features are unusual and the walks make it one of the few created picturesque landscapes in the county.

Postcard from about 1910 showing Glynhir Falls (courtesy of P Davies)

GLYNHIR, Llandybie (SN639151)

Glynhir comprises a small landscape park with associated walled kitchen-garden, dovecote, icehouse, water-management features and picturesque woodland walks dating to the early, mid and late nineteenth century. The water-management features are unusual and the walks make it one of the few created picturesque landscapes in the county.

The Powells are the earliest known family to live at Glynhir; it is thought they built the first mansion, the core of which still survives, in the-mid seventeenth century. Peter du Buisson bought the estate in 1770, and it is probably him or his son, William, who established some of the first garden features that still exist. The du Buisons continued to own the estate until the 1930s. Richard Fenton who visited in 1809 described Glynhir:

> 'Here the Gardens, by being well sheltered, are productive of most excellent fruit. To the South of the House, passing the Gardens, you descend into a deep and beautifully wooded Valley, at least a Mile in length, and crossing a wooden bridge over a deep rocky channel, through which the River takes its course, you turn to the left on the other side, and after crossing a little gulley in the Hill, down which a most picturesque torrent constantly pours'.

It is clear from Fenton's description that by 1809 it was designed in the picturesque style, as understood in the late eighteenth and early nineteenth centuries.

It is not entirely clear what else had been established when Fenton visited, but the Ordnance Survey drawing of 1811 shows what is now the public road (Glynhir Road) to the east of the mansion running through an avenue of trees. Many of these trees still survive in the hedges flanking the road. However, most of what survives seems to have been laid out between the surveying of the parish tithe map in 1841 and the publication of the Ordnance Survey 1:2500 First Edition map in 1877. Indeed much of what is shown on the 1877 map is still in existence or can be traced. Parkland was established to the south and east of the mansion and the area still retains its parkland character. The house may have been approached by a second drive from the north which crosses the river Loughor via a small stone bridge. The gardens to the south and west of the house comprise a lawn with ha-ha, walled garden and orchard.

The Ordnance Survey map also shows a series of sinuous walks leading down the wooded valley to the River Loughor. One of these probably follows the route taken by Richard Fenton in 1809, but the overall pattern is characteristic of a mid-nineteenth century layout. An enigmatic oval enclosure surrounded by a high stone wall stands in the valley woodland, possibly an isolated flower garden similar to the one at Hafod in Ceredigion.

Glynhir is unusual in having had complex water-management and ornamental water features. A leat branching from the River Loughor 1.4km upstream fed these features

Glynhir, near Llandilo.

*The unusual curved canal in front of Glynhir House is shown on this postcard of about 1910
(courtesy of P Davies)*

which included trout ponds, a curved canal to the south of the house and other leats and sluices to provide a head of water to power machinery.

Other notable features include a fine ice-house located 120m to the south-west of the house and an eight-sided dovecote close to the house. The 4m diameter and 6m deep chamber of the ice-house has a domed roof and is reached by a long barrel-vaulted dog-legged stone passage. The roof of the dovecote has collapsed, but bird boxes still line the interior. As well as the buildings and hard landscape features, original planting survives, such as a row of sweet chestnuts planted to commemorate the Battle of Waterloo, a line of lime trees, and a small plantation to the south of the canal planted in the early twentieth century to commemorate four du Buisson children. The parkland retains much of its open character, although invaded by scrub in places, and laurels and rhododendron choke some of the woodland walks.

Glynhir is a Grade II Registered Historic Park and Garden.

Sources:

Cadw: Welsh Historic Monuments, 2002. *Register of Landscapes, Parks and Gardens of Special Historic Interest in Wales. Part 1: Parks and Gardens* (Cardiff: Cadw).

Fisher, J. (ed.), 1917. *Tours in Wales (1804-1813) by Richard Fenton* (London: Cambrian Archaeological Association).

Jones, F., 1987. *Historic Carmarthenshire Homes and their Families* (Carmarthen: Carmarthenshire Antiquarian Society).

Lloyd, T., Orbach, J. and Scourfield, R., 2006. *The Buildings of Wales: Carmarthenshire and Ceredigion* (New Haven: Yale University Press).

Ordnance Survey preliminary drawing of Llandovery by Thomas Budgen of 1811. Digital copy available through the British Library's Online Service.

Old photograph of the waterfall (courtesy of P Davies)

Golden Grove (Gelli Aur)

K Murphy

Founded in the sixteenth century, Golden Grove developed into one of the largest and most important estates in South Wales. Its park and garden was noted for its extensive woodland.

Golden Grove in about 1968 (courtesy of Carmarthenshire Museum)

GOLDEN GROVE, Llanfihangel Aberbythych (SN597199)

Founded in the sixteenth century, Golden Grove developed into one of the largest and most important estates in south Wales. Its park and garden was noted for its extensive woodland, and it still retains an important mid-nineteenth century arboretum. Earlier garden features include an unusual walled garden containing a lake, canal, and a deer park.

Unfortunately at the time of writing Carmarthenshire Record Office was closed and so no use could be made of the vast Golden Grove archive lodged with them. The following is thus based on secondary sources. Note: Golden Grove is the name used on historical documents and maps and is thus preferred to the more recent coinage Gelli Aur.

John Vaughan is credited with building the first Golden Grove on a virgin site in the 1560s. He chose a north-facing slope of the Tywi valley, with the house located close to the valley bottom. By 1670 the house was assessed at 30 hearths, making it with Aberglasney the largest in Carmarthenshire. The form of any gardens that may have accompanied this house is hinted at in documents. Parkland is referred to in 1614 and in a 1686 document *'the free warren and park'* are mentioned'. The warren would have been used for raising rabbits, the earliest mention of such a feature on an estate in Carmarthenshire. Documents of 1714 refer to *'the Old and New Parks'* suggesting that by then one park was of some antiquity and may have been laid out when the house was first built. Another document in the same year states that *'there are woods on the estate fit to be cut down and should have been many years ago'*.

The original house burnt down in 1729 and was not rebuilt until 1754-57, on a site close to the earlier house, by another John Vaughan. The estate had been let for almost 50 years and was in a poor condition, but Vaughan set about with enthusiasm to transform it. From surviving documents it is clear that the parks were heavily wooded and one of Vaughan's first tasks was to clear large tracts of this woodland. To achieve this he entered into an agreement with a timber merchant to sell 3000 oaks in the old park, 640 in the new park, 70 trees in a paddock, 17 oaks out of a copse near the house and 23 elms growing in front of the mansion for the total price of £10,300, a substantial sum in 1757. In addition, the wood by the pond in the lawn was thinned out, but sufficient trees were retained *'as an ornament to ye place'*.

Golden Grove as it is today (photograph: M Ings)

Gardens were laid out *'as a hanging level all the way from the house down to the bottom, with gravelled walks, the whole enclosed'*. Gravelled walks were provided as Vaughan declared himself *'no friend of Green Walks in Wales, where there is so much Rain'*. An icehouse, walled garden and hothouses with vines, peaches and pineapples are recorded, and in 1781 Vaughan built a new hothouse and a *'new circular machine for trimming the edges of Garden Walks'*.

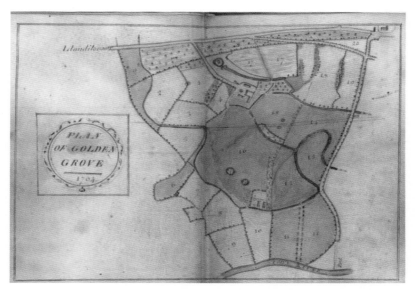

Plan of Golden Grove 1794 showing the house built in 1754-57 and the park and garden surrounding it. Note the pond and canal close to the house and the ox-bow lakes on the Tywi floodplain. North is to the bottom (courtesy of Carmarthenshire Record Office)

Changes and improvements were wrought throughout his lifetime - in 1788 £10 was paid to John Nash to design a cold bath house (there are no records indicating it was built) and in 1790 Vaughan re-planned the garden, paying a Mr Chapman ten guineas for drawing up plans which included conservatories and garden walls partly made of brick from local kilns (a brick and tile works is marked on the Ordnance Survey 1:2500 First Edition map of 1884 a mile to the east of the current house). Several fishponds are recorded and Vaughan built several canals in the vicinity of the house, which were used for keeping fish brought from the *'store pool'* at Bryndu.

However, pike and eels devoured his trout in some of the ponds and so they moved them to the canal in 'Dr Taylor's Walk'. Dr Jeremy Taylor a Royalist clergyman, the *'Shakespeare of the Divines'*, took refuge at Golden Grove in 1645, and according to local tradition he made a daily trip in a rowing boat along a canal from Golden Grove house to his *'Meditation Corner'*. If this is accepted then at least one of the canals predates the late-eighteenth century replanning by over a century.

Despite all this work carried out by John Vaughan some visitors were less than impressed by Golden Grove, for instance Benjamin Malkin writing in 1804 noted: *'I confess myself not a little disappointed on arriving at the place...The house approaches almost to meanness and the situation is flat and low'*.

Golden Grove park and garden as created by John Vaughan is captured on an estate map of 1794 and on the Ordnance Survey preliminary drawing of 1813. Although it is only one inch to a mile the 1813 map is very useful as it shows an arrow-straight public road running from Ffairfach over two miles to the east of Golden Grove to Llanfihangel Aberbythych village immediately to the west, with Golden Grove house in 293 acres (119 ha) of parkland to its north and a larger park of 413 acres (167 ha) labelled 'Golden Grove Park' to its south. It is tempting to suggest that the park to the north is the old park recorded in documents and that to the south the new park. The estate map, reproduced here, shows the park to the north of the road, the house and the walled garden with a pond and canal. Unusually much of the park lies on the floodplain of the Towy, with ox-bow lakes presumably some of the canals or fishponds referred to in historic documents.

John Vaughan died in 1804 and left Golden Grove to his friend Lord Cawdor. Cawdor set about transforming the estate. In 1826-34 a new house in rather harsh grey limestone was built in a more elevated position and the old house was pulled down. The straight road was closed for public use and a new turnpike (the present B4300) constructed along the valley floor to the north of the old house, uniting the two parks. The line of the turnpike road can be seen faintly sketched by an unknown hand on the 1794 estate map. Mr Hill, the long serving gardener of the estate, laid out the gardens from the 1830s onwards. A high stone-built formal terrace was constructed to the south of the house giving extensive views over the Towy valley, and to the north low grassy terraces led up the hillside from the house. In about 1860 an arboretum of some 10.5 acres was planted to the south of the house, separated from the deer park by a ha-ha, and within which was a fernery with a rustic

Golden Grove arboretum as it is today
(photograph: M Ings)

summerhouse. A pinetum was also planted to the south-east of the house. The main drive was (and still is) from the east flanked by an avenue of lime trees. Other drives, each with a lodge, were established to the north, east and south-east, some with subsidiary lodges mid-way along. The area of the 'old' garden underwent considerable modifications and additions during the nineteenth century, but still retained its pond and canal.

The U.S. Air Force occupied the house during the Second World War, and in 1952 Carmarthenshire County Council acquired the lease and used the house and other parts of the estate as an agricultural institute – home farm on the valley floor is now part of Coleg Sir Gâr – and a country park which included the arboretum and the park immediately to the north of the house was established. Much of the park to the south of the house, and large tracts to the north, were planted with conifers. Some large oaks and other trees dating to the Vaughan ownership of the estate survive, as does the walled garden and canal, although the latter is now reduced to a muddy channel. Long stretches of stone wall, now much dilapidated, are probably the last remnants of the Vaughan-period deer park boundaries. In addition to the nineteenth-century arboretum, planting such as holm oaks and monkey-puzzle trees survive in the coniferous forestry. At the time of writing the Golden Grove Trust has plans to restore the house and parts of the park and garden.

The formal terrace at Golden Grove
(courtesy of P Davies)

Golden Grove is a Grade II* Registered Historic Park and Garden.

Sources:

Cadw: Welsh Historic Monuments, 2002. *Register of Landscapes, Parks and Gardens of Special Historic Interest in Wales. Part 1: Parks and Gardens* (Cardiff: Cadw).

Carmarthenshire Record Office, Cawdor/Vaughan mss, Plan of Golden Grove 1794.

Jones, F., 1963, 1964 and 1966. 'The Vaughans of Golden Grove', *Transactions of the Honourable Society of Cymmrodorion.*

Jones, F., 1987. *Historic Carmarthenshire Homes and their Families* (Carmarthen: Carmarthenshire Antiquarian Society).

Lloyd, T., Orbach, J. and Scourfield, R., 2006. *The Buildings of Wales: Carmarthenshire and Ceredigion* (New Haven: Yale University Press).

Llanfihangel Aberbythych Tithe Map and Apportionment 1840. Copy held by Dyfed Archaeological Trust.

Malkin, B. J., 1804. *The Scenery Antiquities and Biography of South Wales* (London: Longman).

Ordnance Survey preliminary drawing of Llanon by Thomas Budgen of 1813. Digital copy available through the British Library's Online Service.

Golden Grove, old postcard (courtesy of P Davies)

Henllys

A Adams Rice

Henllys dates back to the sixteenth century and was once a very
wealthy estate. Within the L-shaped garden, which lies behind the
converted Coach House and barn, is an area of modern paving. There
are young trees and copious herbaceous beds, with a seating area and
ornamental pond.

Henllys House (courtesy of Carmarthenshire Museum)

HENLLYS, Cilycwm (SN754366)

Henllys dates back to the sixteenth century and was once a very wealthy estate, with land on both sides of the River Towy. It lies to the south of Cilycwm village, just north of the market town of Llandovery. Today most of the land has been sold and its core divided into four properties: Henllys Manor House (sometimes known as Henllys Fawr), Henllys Coach House with attached barn, Bailiffs House and Henllys Lodge.

The more frequently used approach is from the north, by a private drive which passes the old lodge then runs down to the old courtyard.

The Coach House (listed Grade II*) is the first building along the drive. It incorporates a former barn (listed Grade II), and courtyard with its utility buildings. Within the L-shaped garden, which lies behind the converted Coach House and barn, is an area of modern paving. There are young trees and copious herbaceous beds, with a seating area and ornamental pond. The back walls have glazed inset lunettes. On the north side of the courtyard are the impressive Grade II listed buildings of stone, with storage bays and six unglazed lunette loft windows. These buildings were built in 1831 for use as cart shed and stables. Below this handsome row is a Dutch hay barn with two full height door openings. The Coach House has a deep luxurious herbaceous planting with a lawned frontage following the line of the façade, only breaking for the wide central entrance arched porch with the date 1829 carved in stone above it. The windows are also arched and a roundel with carved decoration is situated in the gable.

Victorian Lake (photograph: A Adams Rice)

Past Henllys Manor House is a grassed walk to an ornamental lake, recreated on the site of a former Victorian lake in 1995. It has broad walks and boating. The lake is surrounded by a nature reserve of 12 acres of ancient woodland and a further 15 acres of broad leaved woodland planted in 2003.

Between the Coach House and Henllys Manor House is the listed Bailiff's House. This small dwelling is approached from a side track, into an area where the front façade of the elegant Coach House can be seen. The Lodge is at the entrance to the north drive and nestles in an angle between the public road which runs east-west and the drive which runs due south. It has been rebuilt and renovated as a holiday cottage.

Henllys Manor House is a grand double-hipped, five-bay, mansion rebuilt just before the Coach House by the William Jones family. It has a complicated inner roof system and a

Converted Coach House
(photograph: A Adams Rice)

timber Doric porch set on a pair of Roman style columns. The house faces east across the Tywi Valley and is adjacent at a right angle to the Coach House and the smaller listed dwelling known as the Bailiff's House. It has a lawned area below a gravelled frontage.

This area is edged by mature cherry trees and beyond the bottom hedge can be seen the pastureland with ancient oaks that were once owned by the estate. There is a famed 'Lady's Walk' that once left the estate and led to a shaky bridge across two rocks in the river Tywi.

The south-eastern entrance to Henllys estate and its historic buildings is to be found behind Henllys manor house as the drive turns into a curving down-hill restored avenue of young oaks planted during the era of Dutch Elm Disease. This sloping avenue continues in a straightened line until it reaches the pillared main entrance, to the east.

Sources:

Blaenau Tywi History Group, 2014. *Enwau yn y Tirwedd Blaenau Tywi/Names in the Landscape Blaenau Tywi*, (Llandysul: Blaenau Tywi History Group).

Jones, F., 1987. *Historic Carmarthenshire Homes and their Families* (Carmarthen: Carmarthenshire Antiquarian Society).

Lloyd, T., Orbach, J. and Scourfield, R., 2006. *The Buildings of Wales: Carmarthenshire and Ceredigion* (New Haven: Yale University Press).

Notes and photographs taken during meetings and events with Richard and Claire Latimer at Henllys from August 2015. Additional sources from Elizabeth McGill.

Ordnance Survey First Series Edition 1:25000. 1888

2015 tea party held in the garden of Henllys Manor House, on the left with The Bailiff's House and Coach House in the background (photograph: A Adams Rice)

Laugharne Castle

K Murphy

The hard landscaping elements of the gardens of
Laugharne Castle are of some antiquity and include
the picturesque ruined castle itself, crenelated walls
and a gazebo, although many of the softer elements
are restorations of a nineteenth-century layout.

Laugharne Castle (photograph: A Adams Rice)

Arbour at Laugharne Castle (photography: A Adams-Rice)

LAUGHARNE CASTLE, Laugharne (SN302107)

The hard landscaping elements of the gardens of Laugharne Castle are of some antiquity and include the picturesque ruined castle itself, crenelated walls and a gazebo, although many of the softer elements are restorations of a nineteenth-century layout. Some mature trees are present, including a fine Cedar of Lebanon.

Laugharne Castle, overlooking the Tâf estuary, was founded in the early twelfth century during the first phase of the Anglo-Norman conquest of Wales. Originally of timber construction, the castle was rebuilt in stone, with most of the surviving medieval masonry dating to the thirteenth and fourteenth centuries. Its military function declined throughout the medieval period but the buildings were given a new lease of life in the sixteenth century when Sir John Perrot took possession of the castle. He began to transform it into a Tudor mansion but he died before he could complete it. In a survey of 1595 following Perrot's death the following are recorded: *'a little inner courtyard … in the midst of which is a very proper fountaine'*, and *'there is a garden without the court wall of the castle containing by estimation one acre consisting of seven burgages and a half lately built, and taken down which were bought or otherwise taken from the diverse burgesses of the town'*. Traces of the *'fair fountaine'* were discovered during archaeological excavations in the 1970s. Following Perrot's death the castle fell into decline, hastened by it being slighted during the Civil War; it is now a picturesque ruin within the town of Laugharne.

The castle and its grounds came into the ownership of the Starke family, and in about the 1730s they built the first Castle House in what had been the garden created by Sir John Perrot. Elizabeth Ravenscroft inherited the house and castle and in 1798 married Isaac

Starke. They rebuilt Castle House in the grand form visible today, repaired the castle, laid out gardens and added embellishments such as the false crenellations to the tops of walls and a gazebo with views over the estuary. Malkin in his tour of South Wales in 1803 visited the castle and was very critical of the gardens, but he did provide a very useful description:

'the proprietor has laid out the inner court as a modern garden, and in every respect done his utmost to destroy the character of the ruin towards the water. Not only the area, but even one of the towers, is converted to the purposes of horticulture, and filled with the incongruous ornaments of evergreens and flowering shrubs.'

The engraving of the castle accompanying Malkin's description shows Castle House as a low, modest building (unlike the existing house), and the gazebo overlooking the estuary.

Castle House and its garden remain in private hands, but in 1973 Anne Starke placed the castle and its grounds in the care of the Government. The division between Castle House garden and the castle grounds is a high stone wall, the court wall, mentioned in the 1595 survey. Castle House garden has been subdivided, but some early elements survive including a potting shed and glasshouse. Following excavation, conservation of the medieval castle and the restoration of the garden based on its early nineteenth-century layout, the castle and its grounds are now open to the public. Lawns occupy the area to the west of the castle ruins; to the north there is a formal garden parterre of trimmed box hedges enclosing plots each planted with a rose bush. To the north east are winding paths through a shrubbery. There are views over the estuary from the path which runs along the

Formal box hedging, Laugharne Castle (photograph: A Adams Rice)

Sundial over-looking the estuary, Laugharne Castle (photograph: A Adams Rice)

east side of the garden and from the restored gazebo, which is built on the top of a medieval tower. Paths are surfaced with crushed cockle shells, as were the originals – Laugharne is noted for its cockles. Some nineteenth-century planting survives including a Holm oak (*Quercus ilex*), a Cedar of Lebanon (*Cedrus libani*), a sweet chestnut (*Castanea sativa*) and a Turkey oak (*Quercus cerris*). A recent addition is a small arbour commemorating Richard Avent of Cadw who excavated and restored the castle in the 1970s and 1980s. Laugharne Castle is a Grade II Registered Historic Park and Garden.

Sources:

Cadw: Welsh Historic Monuments, 2002. *Register of Landscapes, Parks and Gardens of Special Historic Interest in Wales. Part 1: Parks and Gardens* (Cardiff: Cadw).

Avent, R., 1979. 'Laugharne Castle 1978', *Carmarthenshire Antiquary* 15, 39-56.

Avent, R., 1995. *Laugharne Castle,* (Cardiff: Cadw).

Avent, R, 2006. 'Laugharne Castle'. In: Lloyd, T., Orbach, J. and Scourfield, R. *The Buildings of Wales: Carmarthenshire and Ceredigion* (New Haven: Yale University Press), 219-27.

Malkin, B. J., 1804. *The Scenery Antiquities and Biography of South Wales* (London: Longman.

D Rice Tree Services.

The Castle Lordship and Manor of Tallaugharne otherwise Laugharne with the Members. 2nd October 1595. Original document held by Laugharne Corporation.

CYFFIG DEER PARK, Eglwyscummin (SN222155)

Cyffig Deer Park is included with Laugharne Castle as it was founded by Sir John Perrot, Lord of the Laugharne in the sixteenth century. Perrot was busy transforming Carew Castle and Laugharne Castle from medieval fortresses to Tudor mansions fit for an Elizabethan gentleman and deer parks were a vital element of this transformation. For Laugharne Perrot chose the highest point of the Lordship for his park, eight kilometres north-west of the castle, two-and-a-half kilometres to the south-east of what is now Whitland.

The way that Perrot went about creating his park typifies his approach to life. He did not own all the land he required, so he exchanged some good quality land at St Clears for some poor land at Cyffig in the ownership of one Morgan Phillips. All seemed well, and Perrot set about constructing a pale around what was to be his park. Phillips however, found he had been duped in the exchange, and on the night of the 13th June 1583 set out with 30 men ('*desperate and evill disposed persons*' according to Perrot) and tore down a length of the pale. Perrot re-erected it. It was torn down again, and again re-erected. Eventually a case went to the Star Chamber, who found in Perrot's favour. Following Perrot's death the park was described in a 1595 survey as four miles and three-quarters around containing 300 acres. Perrot's ownership of Laugharne Castle was its last hurrah; it soon fell into disuse and along with it Cyffig Deer Park. Farm names – Old Pale, Great Pale, Little Pale - referring to the pale that once surrounded the park are the only legacy of Perrot's grand creation.

Sources:

Murphy, K., 2009. 'Sir John Perrot's deer park at Cyffig'. In James, H. and Moore, P. (eds) *Carmarthenshire and Beyond: Studies in History and Archaeology in Memory of Terry James* (Carmarthen: Carmarthenshire Antiquarian Society) 231-34.

Laugharne Castle. The gazebo can just be made out in the wall to the right of the castle
(photograph: M Ings)

Llanmiloe House

J Holland

The house is a listed building, and the gardens are included in the Cadw Register of Historic Parks and Gardens as: '*a well preserved Edwardian garden with much original planting*'.

Old postcard of Llanmiloe House garden, early 1900s (courtesy of P Davies)

LLANMILOE HOUSE, Llanddowror (SN248088)

Llanmiloe House is situated 2km east of the village of Pendine, on a south facing slope overlooking West Marsh, Pendine Burrows and the sea. Behind the house the land rises steeply. The woods above the house are known as Coed Llanmiloe, from which the house takes its name. The house is a listed building, and the gardens are included in the Cadw Register of Historic Parks and Gardens as: *'a well preserved Edwardian garden with much original planting'.*

The earliest records for the site refer to an exchange of property between the Cards or Mortimers of Coedmor and Sir John Lewes of Abernant. Rowland Mortimer exchanged Castle Lloyd, to the north-west of the house, for Llanmiloe in 1615. His granddaughter Jane married Owen Edwardes, and the estate passed into the Edwardes family. The old house was demolished and a new Georgian house was built in 1720. In 1830 the house was sold to a relative, William Edwardes, Second Lord Kensington. The transaction was not completed until 1837. He sold it on to Morgan Jones in the 1840s. It then remained in the Jones family until 1941 when it was compulsorily purchased by the military.

The estate in 1873 is recorded as 11,031 acres with 80 acres of formal gardens and woodland. A roof terrace and garden above the house is also recorded. It is not known when these were created, or if they survive.

The main core of the house was enlarged in the late 1800s by the addition of an east wing, and a further extension was added to the west in 1905-1908. The house is roughcast render over stone and is painted a pale cream colour. The central block is three storeys while the two flanking extensions are two-storey. The front of the house has a central classical square porch, with a moulded cornice and Roman Doric columns.

The Edwardian garden was laid out during this period of expansion. A new drive, which has two red-stone pillars at the entrance, was added to the west of the house, it passes a lodge house on the right, and then curves round to the east towards the west end of the house. There is a large forecourt at the front of the house. The lodge remains largely unaltered, and has been occupied by the same couple since 1952. The original gates have been replaced by modern ones.

The new drive was lined with plane trees, but these have now gone. There are still a number of mature trees on both sides of the drive. The grounds to the south of the house were laid out around 1908 to create four grassed terraces, with red-stone steps providing access between them. The top three flights are placed centrally rising to the house, the bottom terrace has steps at both ends to the east and west. To the east of the lower terrace was a rose garden. To the west are the tennis courts, and areas of lawn. The grounds below the house are extensively planted with woody exotics and rhododendrons. These include a number of rhododendrons, a lime, a Monterey cypress, a cedar, horse and sweet chestnuts and a number of walnut trees.

The original drive approached the house from the east via the coach house and stable block. The coach house was demolished in the 1950s and the stables have recently been converted into holiday accommodation. To the east of the house were the orchards and kitchen gardens. These have since been built on. No glasshouses are shown on the First Edition Ordnance Survey map, but the resident in the lodge recalls an extensive lean-to greenhouse, which was demolished to make room for the prefabricated buildings to the east. The Cadw Register describes a garden to the north of the house, which was a small secluded garden. This may have been used as a nursery garden for the house. Above the house in the woods to the north-east was a small dam and reservoir, which provided water for the house, and was channelled via a series of small ponds and a 4m waterfall through the grounds.

Today a lot of clearance work is going on in the grounds, with a number of large trees being felled. There is no evidence of a garden behind the house, and the rose garden no longer exists.

The family remained at Llanmiloe until 1941 when it was purchased by the military. During the early 1940s prefabricated bungalows were built to the south east and south west of the

Old postcard of Llanmiloe House and gardens (courtesy of P Davies)

house. A welfare centre and church were added. The land to the south of the main road was used by the military as experimental ranges. The house became the headquarters and officers mess.

After the war the Armament Development Board decided that Pendine would be retained as a permanent military establishment. Part of the marsh was reclaimed to provide a sports field for cricket and football, with a bowling green. By the 1950s there was a thriving community with 2000 personnel based at Pendine. Llanmiloe House was kept as the headquarters. The military continued to maintain the grounds.

By 1997, with the defence budget being cut, the Ministry of Defence moved out of the area and the ranges were taken over by QinetQ, a defence technology company. Llanmiloe House remained empty for five years before being sold. The bungalows either side were handed over to the Welsh Government, knocked down and replaced by more modern housing. The house and grounds now nestle between two housing developments, with an extensive caravan park along the coast to the west.

Llanmiloe is a Grade II Registered Historic Park and Garden.

Sources:

Cadw: Welsh Historic Monuments, 2002. *Register of Landscapes, Parks and Gardens of Special Historic Interest in Wales. Part 1: Parks and Gardens* (Cardiff: Cadw).

Jones, F., 1987. *Historic Carmarthenshire Homes and their Families* (Carmarthen: Carmarthenshire Antiquarian Society).

Steps at Llanmiloe House
(photograph: courtesy G Hudson)

Llechdwnni

K Murphy

Llechdwnni's history stretches back into the medieval period, and an old ruined house and an unusual walled garden indicate its high status in the seventeenth century.

1985 aerial photograph of Llechdwnni (courtesy of Dyfed Archaeological Trust)

LLECHDWNNI, Llandyfaelog (SN428100)

Llechdwnni is now a working farm, with a modest-sized Victorian farmhouse. However, its history stretches back into the medieval period, and an old ruined house and an unusual walled garden indicate its high status in the seventeenth century.

The early history of the site is unclear, but Francis Jones records that several generations of the Donne (or Dwnn) family lived at Llechdwnni until it passed into the ownership of the Bowens in the early sixteenth century. Mary Bowen married John Brigstocke in 1626. The Brigstocke family continued to own Llechdwnni until they sold it in 1909, but during the eighteenth century and later it was let to tenants. A triptych by Hans Memling of the Virgin and Child commissioned by Sir John Donne of Kidwelly in about 1478 now hangs in the National Gallery in London and attests the wealth of the Donne family at that time. However, the remains of Llechdwnni garden and old house are ascribed to the Brigstocks in the seventeenth century.

The small old house stands to the north of the present house and is now used as a farm outbuilding. It probably dates to the early seventeenth century, but may contain earlier elements. To the west is the walled garden. This is square, of approximately two acres, with walls of stone rubble faced on the inside with hand-made bricks. At the west end the garden rises steeply onto an eight-metre wide terrace flanked by semi-circular walls projecting out from the north-west and south-west corners of the garden walls. These are the foundations of belvederes or gazebos giving panoramic views over the surrounding countryside.

The interior of the walled garden is now grassed over, as is a small enclosure to the north of the old house, which may have been an orchard or garden. The Ordnance Survey 1:2500 First Edition map of 1890 shows formal paths and fruit trees here. A rectangular pond now choked with rushes lies outside the walled garden to the west and probably had an ornamental function. A larger rectangular pond is shown on the Ordnance Survey 1811 preliminary drawing and on the First Edition map to the east of the current and old house. It is now virtually gone and it is unclear whether this, too, had an ornamental function.

Llechdwnni is a Grade II Registered Historic Park and Garden.

Sources:

Cadw: Welsh Historic Monuments, 2002. *Register of Landscapes, Parks and Gardens of Special Historic Interest in Wales. Part 1: Parks and Gardens* (Cardiff: Cadw).
Jones, F., 1987. *Historic Carmarthenshire Homes and their Families* (Carmarthen: Carmarthenshire Antiquarian Society).
Ordnance Survey preliminary drawing of Carmarthen by Thomas Budgen of 1811. Digital copy available through the British Library's Online Service.

Llwynywormwood

J Holland

Llwynywormwood (now renamed Llwynywermod) was
designed as a parkland landscape in the late eighteenth/ early
nineteenth century.

Watercolour of the old house, now a ruin (courtesy The National Library of Wales)

LLWYNYWORMWOOD, Myddfai (SN769315)

Llwynywormwood (now renamed Llwynywermod) was designed as a parkland landscape in the late eighteenth/early nineteenth century. It was created with three sweeping drives approaching the house from the north, south and east, so that views of the countryside might be enjoyed on approaching the house, with perhaps the occasional glimpse of the house through the trees. The mansion house looks north across the park, over a lake and stream, to the hills of the Brecon Beacons in the distance. Both the First Edition and Second Edition Ordnance Survey maps (1886 and 1906) show the mansion house, lake, farm buildings and walled garden.

There were four distinct periods of occupation, starting with a homestead, followed in the late eighteenth/early nineteenth century by the mansion, which is now a ruin, and later in the 1860s by the conversion of the stables and farm buildings into a farmhouse. The barn which forms part of the farm buildings is Grade II listed. Recent restoration of the estate by the Duchy of Cornwall is the fourth and final period.

The earliest homestead, of which only a portion remains, dates to the medieval period. This was incorporated into the mansion as an outside kitchen or bake house. The homestead was occupied by the Williams family until 1785. The estate was then left to a nephew, George Griffies.

George Griffies (Williams) built the mansion house between 1785 and 1809. It sits on a level platform looking north across the estate. The house is aligned north/south and was

The ruins of Llwynywormwood (photograph: E Whittle)

Ruins of the original mansion (photograph: E Whittle)

bay fronted with a number of chimneys and a belvedere. One of the bays on the front later became a conservatory. There was a ha-ha on the north side and what may have been a rectangular ice-house, cut into the bedrock, which may have been supplied with ice from a small pond near the house. George also added the farm buildings a short distance to the south-east. These were constructed on four sides of a small courtyard and include a large barn on one side. Further to the south-west, a walled garden was added which forms part of three enclosures. The enclosures may have included a vegetable garden and orchard. There is no evidence for a formal garden, lawns or beds. A pencil and ink drawing of Llwynywormwood, in the collection of the National Library of Wales, shows the house sitting within the landscape. The ha-ha which ran along the front of the house would indicate that the house was designed to be a part of the larger landscape with uninterrupted views of the countryside beyond.

The parkland was designed to include scattered groups of trees, drives to be enjoyed from a carriage, with scenic views, meandering paths, ornamental lodges, and bridges over the stream. The landscape was crossed by three drives coming in from Llandovery in the north, Myddfai to the south, and past Penhill Lodge from the east. The stream, the Nant Ydw, was dammed to create a lake, and was crossed by two bridges. There were paths across the park, one of which dropped down to the lake, and across the stream. There were five lodges, only two of which remain: the Round Lodge and Penhill Lodge. The Round lodge was an eight-sided building on a bend of the north drive. Elisabeth Whittle (Register of Landscapes, Parks and Gardens of Special Interest: in Wales: Part I: Parks and Gardens) describes this as an eye -catcher, built as much to create a tableau as a functional lodge to the main entrance of the house, as was fashionable at the time.

As early as 1809 Richard Fenton describes the landscape: *'charming situation, grounds very parkish ornamented with fine masses of old wood. To the back a noble view of the Mountains, which from hence look like the view of Cader Idris softened and in miniature '.*To have achieved this the parkland may have been laid out some years earlier for the stands of oak to have reached maturity. This, perhaps, even predates the building of the mansion, which is dated around 1785- 1809. At its height the estate enjoyed shooting over some 4000 acres and included thirty one properties.

In 1831 the house was advertised to let in the Cambrian as a *'well furnished ...delightfully situated mansion of eight bedroom chambers, besides servants rooms and suitable offices, roomy coach house, stabling for nine horses, greenhouse adjoining the house....also very good walled and other gardens'.*

When Sir George Griffies died in 1843 the estate passed to Revd Erasmus Henry Griffies-Williams. He did not live at Llwynywormwood. He was Chancellor of St Davids from 1858 until his death in 1871. The property was let in his absence to a number of tenants including Captain Alfred Crawshay, mentioned in The Welshman in 1853 as one of the landowners who approved the Vale of Towy Railway line, and the infamous Revd G Bree, who broke the rental agreement and disappeared to New Zealand owing Griffies-Williams rent. There is an advertisement in The Welshman, prior to the Revd Bree's departure, for two ponies and a recently repaired elegantly fashioned phaeton. Also advertised for sale was a water-wheel 12 foot in diameter.

Despite being an absentee landlord for much of this time, Revd Erasmus Henry Griffies-Williams took a keen interest in farming. It was reported that he brought farm machinery from Wiltshire to be demonstrated at the Llandovery Agricultural Society ploughing match in 1841.

When he died the property passed, via his brother General Watkin Lewis Griffies-Williams, to his two daughters: Juliana, who died in 1884, and Caroline who died in 1907. Published in The Welshman 6 August 1875, the *'Messuage or Mansion House called Llwynywormwood Park '* was described as including the mansion, *'together with the gardens, pleasure grounds, woods and lands adjoining.... altogether 5900 acres'.* The estate went through turbulent times in the hands of the executors and parts were sold off in 1879, 1909 and 1912. As can be seen from a number of advertisements in the local papers, the estate sold quantities of timber during this period, predominantly larch and oak.

Llwynywormwood was sold in 1913 and again in 1960. During the Second World War the estate was used as a training centre for the Home Guard, and for infantry gunnery practise. Up until this point the house had been habitable, but during this period it was badly vandalised. In 1963 the estate was again sold, and purchased by the Strouds. They fenced off the house, filled in the ha-ha and took down the old conservatory. Much of the mansion was then demolished and its stone reused on the estate.

In 1998 Llwynywormwood was bought by John and Patricia Hegarty. They moved into the old three-bay coach house and loft and started to restore the estate. They restored the walled garden, and experimented in growing crops along modern scientific lines. In 2001 they were granted planning permission to restore the lake, which had become badly silted up, but this was never done. In 2006 after living there for nine years they sold the estate to the Duchy of Cornwall. It now comprises 192 acres of which 150 are grazed parkland and 40 acres are woodland.

Since then, the estate has been extensively restored. The farm buildings, with the coach house at the front, a pair of two bedroom cottages on the west side, and the great barn along the south side, form a square with a courtyard in the middle. The emphasis has been on the employment of local craftsmen and the use of Welsh materials. The courtyard has original cobble paths, and has been planted as a cottage garden, with herbs and flowers in square beds. There are climbing roses on the walls. At the front of the building is a rectangular garden, with beds and a lawn fenced within a rustic timber enclosure. The Prince of Wales' crest of three feathers is carved into the gate. The six field maples that lined Westminster Abbey in 2011 for the wedding of Prince William and Kate Middleton have been replanted in the garden.

An orchard of pear trees has been planted for juice, to be sold by the estate. The meadow between the house and the walled garden has been seeded as a wild flower meadow by spreading meadow hay cut and brought from the pasture of the Royal estate at Highgrove in Gloucestershire. Already wild orchids are establishing and the grass is a sea of colour in early summer, with oxeye daisies, yellow rattle and poppies.

The half- acre walled garden, restored by the Hegartys, is a surprising distance from the ruined mansion, sited above it and near the south boundary of the park. It is rectangular with rounded corners, on a sloping site. There is a window in one of the walls. The main entrance is in the south wall, with another in the north-west corner. A small orchard has been planted in part of the walled garden, the rest grassed.

The lake has not been restored, but the substantial dam remains and the island is still visible as an area of slightly higher ground with a patch of rhododendrons.

The Estate is not open to the public, but the cottages are rented out for holidays when the Royal Family are not in residence. Today it is a quiet peaceful place, with beautiful views over rolling parkland to the mountains in the distance. It remains a picturesque landscape, with grassland dotted with groups of mature trees.

Llwynywormwood is a Grade II Registered Historic Park and Garden.

Sources:

Baker, M., 2008. A Royal Home in Wales: Llwynywermod, (Bedlinog: Accent Press).

Cadw: Welsh Historic Monuments, 2002. *Register of Landscapes, Parks and Gardens of Special Historic Interest in Wales. Part 1: Parks and Gardens* (Cardiff: Cadw).

First and Second Edition Ordnance Survey 1:2500 maps.

Fisher, J. (ed.), 1917. *Tours in Wales (1804-1813) by Richard Fenton* (London: Cambrian Archaeological Association).

Guided tour of the grounds by the Estate Manager in 2013.

Jones, F., 1987. *Historic Carmarthenshire Homes and their Families* (Carmarthen: Carmarthenshire Antiquarian Society).

Lloyd, T., Orbach, J. and Scourfield, R., 2006. *The Buildings of Wales: Carmarthenshire and Ceredigion* (New Haven: Yale University Press).

National Library of Wales, photographic collections.

RCAHMW, pictures and records in the National Monument Record, Aberystwyth.

Maesycrugiau Manor

J Holland

Maesycrugiau Manor is a
Grade II listed house
and registered historic
park and garden 1.5
miles south of the village
of Maesycrugiau. The
register entry mentions
'the remains of an
extraordinary Edwardian
summerhouse in a
somewhat neglected
contemporary garden'.

Ornamental lily pond

(courtesy M Van Ostade)

MAESYCRUGIAU MANOR, Llanllwni (SN477404)

Maesycrugiau Manor is a Grade II listed house and registered historic park and garden 1.5 miles south of the village of Maesycrugiau. The register entry mentions *'the remains of an extraordinary Edwardian summerhouse in a somewhat neglected contemporary garden'*.

There was an earlier house on this site which may date back to the Elizabethan period. In the garden are some steps, going down from the main terrace to the garden below, which may date to this period. The Mansel family called them the Elizabethan steps.

Francis Jones mentions the Lloyds as *'the first family of note'* to live here and the family pedigree and arms were recorded by Dwnn in 1609. The property was inherited by the Thomas family and later, by marriage in 1878, passed to Sir Richard Mansel. The house remained in the Mansel family until 1994 when the estate was sold to become a country club and restaurant. The grandson of Sir Courtenay Mansel still lives nearby.

The earlier house burnt down on the 28 January 1902. Stone was salvaged from the burnt remains and one of the walls was re-used in the construction of the new house which was built between 1903 and 1904 for Sir Courtney Mansel. The house was designed by Arnold Mitchell. An artist's impression and the architect's drawings were reproduced in *The English Home of Today* in 1904. The plans show an extensive house on two sides of a court, with a library, hall or ballroom, and drawing room with two bays. The wing containing the library and ballroom was never completed. On the west front the keystones for the missing wing can be still be seen, and internally there is a staircase leading to a blank wall which would have led to the gallery above the library. There were other economies, including the reduction from three lanterns to one, in the ceiling marked kitchen on the plan. The house has a large and imposing square tower and is built in an impressive style with a number of substantial chimneys. It was built to incorporate the latest in modern amenities, including a heating system.

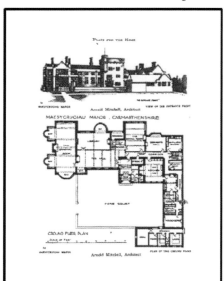

Artists impression of the house and floor plan. The ballroom and library were never completed (extract from 'The English Home of Today')

Sir Courtenay Mansel redesigned the garden about the same time as the new house was built in 1903-04. The Ordnance Survey map of 1891 shows the main entrance to the house from the west, towards the railway station, with a tree-lined avenue, and two other carriage drives to the east and a walled garden to the east of the house. This was divided into four quadrants with a circular feature in the centre, which may have been an ornamental pond.

*An extraordinary summer house with camera obscura at
Maesycrugiau (photograph: J Holland; plan courtesy of
The Museum of English Rural Life)*

There are formal walks through the grounds which are extensively wooded with both conifer and broad-leaved trees. By 1905, only the outline of the walled garden remained: it had been replaced by a levelled area which the family used for tennis. The 1905 Ordnance Survey map shows a fourth drive to the north-east, which had been planted with an avenue of trees and appears to be the main entrance at this time. By this stage the outlying fields had also been planted with clumps of broad-leaved trees and conifers; these have now been removed.

Today the main entrance is from the east, with the large pond on the left of the drive and the remains of the walled garden on the right hand side. The drive sweeps round to the right, the house only visible as the drive opens out in front of it. The drive to the west has been lost, as the land has been sold off, and the once elegant wrought iron gates and posts on that side have disappeared.

There is a terrace to the south of the house which is thought to be contemporary with the earlier house. Below that the lower garden is divided into three sections linked by steps. There is a formal garden, re-created in the last 15 years by the current owners, Mr and Mrs Mark Van Ostade, on what was the car park to the country hotel. It has clipped box hedging in a circular geometric design, a rectangular raised pond, and an area of lawn. A concrete rill runs diagonally through the formal garden to feed the pond. This is backed by mature yews which are planted in a geometric design. Initially standing only a few feet high and neatly clipped, the pattern would have been clear from the ground. Today the yews stand as mature overgrown trees. There are two large oaks on either side of the house. There are also some ancient Japanese cedars (*Crytomeria japonica*), and Western Red cedars (*Thuja plicata*) and a couple of Japanese maples (*Acer japonica*)

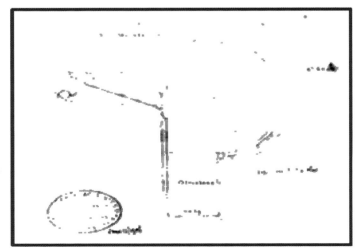

*The 'Elizabethan Steps' at Maesycrugiau
(photograph: J Holland)*

which are recent introductions. Although the house is surrounded by mature trees, and is invisible from the east, its main rooms look out over the rolling countryside into the distance.

Maesycrugiau is translated as the field of small hillocks or tumuli. Today there is a single mound or tumulus to the right of the main drive. This is not considered to be a burial mound, but may have been a garden feature, or viewing platform, used in the laying out of the earlier garden.

Described in the Cadw Register Entry as an 'Extraordinary Edwardian summer house' is a tower or belvedere standing about 10.5 metres high. This would have commanded, from its elevated position, extensive views all around, but today is surrounded by mature trees. At its foot is a rounded red stone walled structure about a metre high, with two rectangular extensions leading from the circle. The belvedere is recorded in the Register as having two towers; the circular structure was thought to be a pond with water lilies at eye level. Plans for this structure were discovered amongst the papers of the Messenger Heating Company, who were engaged by the Mansels in 1906 to provide a heating system for the pavilion and glasshouse.

The original plans from the Messenger papers show a rounded structure with two extensions leading from it (illustration). The drawings are marked: glass house, pavilion and camera obscura.

The camera obscura tower which is five-sided at the base, has a stone core and is topped with an eight sided wooden room with windows all round. This contained the camera or lenses of a camera obscura. Using mirrors, as in an 18th-century overhead version, it is possible to project an image the right-side-up. Light from an external scene passes through the hole and strikes a surface inside, where it is reproduced, rotated 180 degrees . This reflects the colours and image enabling the artist to reproduce them in perspective.

It is not clear whether Messenger & Co completed the glasshouse. There is a bill for the greenhouse and additions to the pavilion in their archive, and the diagram shows a stove house, boiler and pipework. The heating system was installed and paid for in 1906. There is a letter from Sir Courtenay Mansel, not dated, which mentions the possibility *'to tender for another job shortly'*. Almost one hundred years later, with the plans, it was possible to identify the features on the ground. The tower and the stone walls of the base of the pavilion and greenhouse remain, and parts of the tiled floor can still be seen in the grass.

The house today is a small country hotel. In 2015 it was for sale with seven acres of grounds.

Maesycrugiau is a Grade II Registered Historic Park and Garden.

Sources:

British Newspaper Archive.

Cadw: Welsh Historic Monuments, 2002. *Register of Landscapes, Parks and Gardens of Special Historic Interest in Wales. Part 1: Parks and Gardens* (Cardiff: Cadw).

Jones, F., 1987. *Historic Carmarthenshire Homes and their Families* (Carmarthen: Carmarthenshire Antiquarian Society).

Lloyd, T., Orbach, J. and Scourfield, R., 2006. *The Buildings of Wales: Carmarthenshire and Ceredigion* (New Haven: Yale University Press).

Museum of English Rural Life, letters, plans, and invoices from the Messenger papers. National Library of Wales, photographic collections.

Notes taken from meeting with Marc Van Ostade June 2015.

Ordnance Surveys First and Second Edition 1:2500 maps.

Shaw Sparrow, W. (ed.), 1904. *The British Home of Today: A Book of Modern Domestic Architecture and Applied Arts*, (Hodder & Stoughton London).

The remains of the Pavilion base (photograph: J Holland)

Middleton Hall

National Botanical Garden of Wales

R Thomas

For the first ten years of its existence as the National Botanic Garden of Wales little was known of the earliest origins of the 568 acre estate that it occupies. Understandable really, as much of the initial effort was geared to creating a modern, sustainable and new national garden for the twenty-first century.

Thomas Hornor's 1815 painting of Middleton Hall (courtesy of the National Botanic Garden of Wales. Reproduced by kind permission of the Grant family)

MIDDLETON HALL – NATIONAL BOTANIC GARDEN OF WALES, Llanarthne (SN522181)

For the first ten years of its existence as the National Botanic Garden of Wales little was known of the earliest origins of the 568 acre estate that it occupies. Understandable really, as much of the initial effort was geared to creating a modern, sustainable and new national garden for the twenty-first century. Gardens take time to grow and as the iconic Carmarthenshire destination matured, attention did, naturally and eventually, turn to a more systematic investigation of the past and a renewed vigour in honouring the all-encompassing vision of the Garden's initiators and founders. The discoveries were remarkable, highly serendipitous and served to underpin the international credentials, not only of the Garden itself, but also a landscape that had remained substantially unspoilt for the best part of half a millennium. They served too, to pave the way for the future.

Middleton Hall
(courtesy of Carmarthenshire Museum)

The eponymous Middletons can first be traced to Llanarthne when, in February 1584, Christopher Middleton was appointed local vicar. There are, however, mentions of Middletons in and around Carmarthenshire from the middle of the sixteenth century. First, Fulke Middleton is recorded as Alderman of Carmarthen, followed by his son, Edward, in 1575, who went on to become mayor in 1583. Edward was a cousin to Christopher Middleton and the latter was, by 1609, paying a land fee to the Duchy of Lancaster equivalent to a holding of around 500 acres. Is it more than coincidence that this is similar in size to the parkland the Garden occupies today?

Speculation aside, this does beg a question as to how Christopher, as vicar of a modest, rural parish, was able to appear the second largest local landholder after the Vaughans of Golden Grove. The answer to this would seem to rest with the wider family network and the significant inroads it was making into the upper echelons of society. In short, the Middletons comprised a family 'on the make'. Springing from a comparatively modest farmhouse at Galch Hill in Denbighshire the family's eminence grew in very short order to see members at the head of the London guilds, acting as county high sheriffs, powerful business influencers, MPs and ultimately, in the case of Sir Thomas Myddelton, Lord Mayor of London.

A prime example of the Middletons being at the forefront of things was the attendance of several of them at a historic meeting at Founders Hall in Lothbury Street, London, in September 1599. There, prime movers at the heart of the capital's commercial fortunes resolved to petition the Queen for the charter that was to lead to the creation of the East India Company, a venture that was to become the powerhouse driving the creation of empire and to endure for more than 250 years.

John, Henry and David were Christopher Middleton's elder brothers and for the first decade of the 17th century their flames burned bright. John captained one of the vessels on the Company's inaugural expedition and the three were involved in all of its early voyages, with Henry later knighted for his services. The wealth the brothers amassed was fabulous but, as was often the case with this early generation of merchant adventurers, life was brutal, with all three succumbing to the occupational hazards of tropical disease or drowning by 1615.

Thomas Hornor's painting of Middleton Hall (courtesy of The National Botanic Garden of Wales. Reproduced by kind permission of the Grant family)

So what are the implications of all this for a few hundred acres of parkland in the country? Sir Henry's account books show that there was a close business relationship between him and his younger brother Christopher and testify to Henry's wider ownership of local lands. It seems that between around 1605 and 1612, the year before his death, he either owned outright or had a significant interest in Dinefwr Castle. It also seems reasonable to posit, at least, that it was via Christopher that funds from David and Henry were being channelled to create a junior version of what the more senior Myddeltons had achieved at Chirk Castle and Stanstead Hall in Essex: that is to say the sort of country estate to which men of enterprise were beginning to aspire. From the wills of both David and Sir Henry it is apparent that the future fortunes of this branch of the Middletons were vested in David's son, also called Henry, who by 1644 was High Sheriff of Carmarthen and residing at Middleton Hall, Llanarthne.

Modest archaeological investigations in 2011 and 2012 confirmed the existence of a significant dwelling at the heart of the estate, almost certainly the Llanarthne home that is recorded as paying tax on 17 hearths in 1676. This was flanked by formal gardens and water features and consistent with early Jacobean taste and fashion. Intriguingly, the investigations also hinted at earlier evidence of occupation, which would suggest, not uncommonly, that Carmarthen incomers, the Middletons, were enhancing and embellishing structures that pre-dated their arrival.

For a modern, national botanic garden these discoveries have major, if coincidental significance. Indicating a heritage inextricably linked with plants for health, economic botany and the enduring exploitation of natural resources in fighting disease provides a rich seam of narratives to engage, educate and entertain the visitor. It also confers on a young garden credentials that enable it to stand comparison with peers that have been in existence for many hundreds of years.

If it can be accepted that the Garden's estate has existed for the best part of 500 years, then it has passed through comparatively few hands in that time. In Middleton ownership for perhaps 170 years, little record of the estate remains, but its heyday and full flourishing is well documented and depicted. In the late 1780s Middleton Hall was purchased by William (later Sir William) Paxton, recently returned from overseas venturing and an archetypal nabob. The path he had trodden to success and immense wealth was in many respects no different from that of the Middletons – comparatively humble origins, a career at sea (Paxton was a midshipman at 14) and enrichment through service with the East India Company and private enterprise. Paxton may have been aware of the estate's heritage, too, and the resonance of the Middleton name – he had counted a Middleton descendant, Nathaniel, as a private client in India. He retained the name when he built his new mansion and it is perhaps no accident that Paxton's Tower, the folly that overlooks the Tywi Valley is dedicated to another, more famous seaman, Nelson.

Thomas Hornor's 1815 painting of the lake, Middleton Hall (courtesy of the National Botanic Garden of Wales. Reproduced by kind permission of the Grant family)

Paxton set about a root and branch reshaping of the landscape in the taste and fashion of the time, employing some of the finest minds of his generation. Samuel Pepys-Cockerell, the architect of a number of the grand residences commissioned by the nabobs, designed the new hall; James Grier provided the engineering input to create the artificial necklace of lakes that circled the hill on which the hall stood and, it has been suggested, Samuel Lapidge, inheritor of Capability Brown's mantle, landscaped the grounds. Whilst this last point is unproven, it is known from Paxton's correspondence that he was acquainted with Samuel Lapidge.

What the combination of talents created was *'one of the best built and most magnificent house in Wales'* (Lipscomb 1802) and a park *'richly ornamented by nature, greatly improved by art'* (sale catalogue 1824), which responded to the neo-classical aesthetic inspired by Claude Lorraine and Poussin. This was, moreover, a designed landscape that lent itself naturally to shifts in taste and fashion and there is evidence within the park today of changes effected during Paxton's time to reflect this. As the landscape unfolds, the rationalism of the neo-classical gives way to a more sombre mood, more experiential and irregular in form, colour, lighting and sound responding more closely to the later Romantic and Picturesque aesthetic. This is the achievement that is tellingly recorded by the watercolours that Paxton commissioned from Thomas Hornor in 1815. A surveyor by training, Hornor worked extensively in south Wales, characterising himself a *'Pictural Delineator of Estates'*, offering an *'improved'* style of drawing greatly enhanced by what he called *'panoramic chorometry'*.

Thomas Horner's painting of Middleton Hall (courtesy of the National Botanic Garden of Wales. Reproduced by kind permission of the Grant family)

Critically, for the Garden today and for the future, the landscape that Hornor depicted, the subject of a steady decline and benign neglect that have endured for more than a century, is not beyond recapture and restoration and that, indeed, is the ambition. The Garden was originally conceived as a harmonious blend of the old and the new, with Lord Norman Foster's *'elliptical torus'*, the iconic Great Glasshouse, nestling comfortably in the landscape alongside the surviving structures of Paxton's Middleton Hall. Just as what was to become the largest single-span glasshouse in the world was created, other rarities were restored to complement the whole, most notably perhaps the Double Walled Garden. Now a Systematics Garden, interpreting the latest understanding of genetic inter-relationships between plants, this was originally a working garden providing the estate with an abundance of fresh fruit and vegetables. Its double walls, the outer of stone, the inner of brick, served the dual functions of protecting crops against the prevailing westerlies and retaining heat to extend growing seasons and create a micro-climate that allowed tender plants to flourish. It's not hard to imagine Paxton impressing his guests with a harvest of unseasonably early strawberries or late cropped peaches.

If the Double Walled Garden today is much as it was in the middle of the eighteenth century, that is not to say that there haven't been casualties, too. The Great Glasshouse today sits on the site of what was an ornamental fountain, flanked by paths and associated plantings. This is depicted in the illustrations of Augustus Butler of the 1850s and may well have been an introduction effected by Edward Hamlin Adams who purchased the estate after Paxton's death in 1824. These garden elements were almost certainly early victims of the neglect that followed the disastrous house fire of 1931.

Times change and people, too, up to a point, but Paxton's landscape was created to be enjoyed. Even though we live through times that offer bewildering ranges of digital diversions (and there is scope for those aplenty at the Garden, too), there is much to recommend traditional pastimes and pursuits and genuine experiences in traditional, restored settings. This is a critical impetus behind the Garden's ambition to complete the work that was started in the mid 1990s and to achieve a large-scale landscape restoration that will see the re-introduction of the impressive network of lakes, waterfall, dams, cascades, weirs and designed plantings that so enchanted visitors more than 200 years ago.

The Garden has a 1,000 year lease on the land it occupies and, bolstered by a better understanding of its 500 year inheritance, it is laying the foundations for future generations, importantly from all walks of life, to enjoy much of what Sir William Paxton's family and friends enjoyed so many years before.

Middleton Hall is a Grade II Registered Historic Park and Garden.

The Great Glass House, National Botanic Garden Of Wales. Tree stump in the foreground - a modern fashion statement after the stumpery at Highgrove (photograph: M Ings)

Nelson's (Paxton's) Tower

K Murphy

Nelson's Tower now more commonly known as Paxton's Tower is one of the best known and most prominent follies in Wales. It is included here because of its picturesque character and on account of its connection with the Middleton Hall Estate.

Nelson's (Paxton's) Tower from the southeast. The line of the spiral carriage drive can be made out below the wooden fence (photograph: M Ings)

NELSON'S TOWER/PAXTON'S TOWER, Llanarthne (SN540191)

Nelson's Tower, now more commonly known as Paxton's Tower, is one of the best known and most prominent follies in Wales. It is included here because of its picturesque character and on account of its connection with the Middleton Hall estate.

Sir William Paxton commissioned the architect Samuel Pepys-Cockrell to design a tower dedicated to his friend Lord Nelson. It was built in 1808. There are many tales related as to why Paxton built the tower, the most frequently told being that he built it in fit of pique and that he wanted to demonstrate his continuing wealth after failing to get elected to Parliament despite spending lavishly to buy the votes of his constituents.

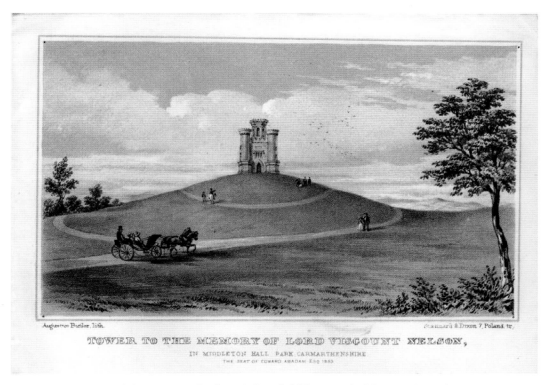

Lithograph by Augustus Butler, 1853, titled 'Tower to the Memory of Lord Viscount Nelson in Middleton Hall Park, Carmarthenshire. Note the carriage drive spiralling up the hill.

The Tower is triangular in plan, three storeys high with round angle turrets and topped with a hexagonal turret. Essentially it was an eye catcher located on a hill above Paxton's Middleton Hall estate, but it also had what was described as a sumptuous banqueting hall on the first floor, from which wide ranging views over Carmarthenshire and beyond were obtained. The original way to the tower was from the north along a carriage drive leading diagonally up the steep valley side of the river Tywi. A circular lodge lay alongside this drive 200m to the west of the Tower and 40m below it, where woodland gives way to the grass-

Old postcard (courtesy P Davies)

covered hilltop. The sharp-eyed visitor glimpses the top crenelations of the Tower from here, but immediately on progressing, the view of the tower is lost by the bulk of the hill as the drive curves around to the north and then to the west, and a full view of the tower is not obtained until the drive turns to the south, to the west of the tower. At this point the top of the hill is still 10m higher up, but the drive does not lead there directly, but continues its gently spiralling course. Panoramic views are not obtained until the drive reaches the east and north side of the hilltop. The drive then continues, eventually arriving at the base of the Tower on its west side. At this point the drive spreads out into a wide platform, where carriages could have been turned and then driven into the ground-floor of the tower through one of the three arched openings. This drive is a classic Picturesque device, by which the visitor is slowly rewarded for his or her effort, rather than everything being revealed at once. The earthworks of the drive spiralling around the hill are still easily traceable; the circular lodge is reduced to low stone walls.

The circular lodge is one of two shown on a sale plan of the Middleton Estate of 1824, the second lying 150m to the south-west of the tower. The circular lodge is named 'Tower Lodge' on the 1888 Ordnance Survey 1:2500 map, however the lodge to the west had been by then converted to a farm, called Towerhill Farm. All had changed by the publication of the 1906 map: the circular lodge had been abandoned and what had been Towerhill Farm had been renamed Tower Lodge. This building is now a single-storey cottage owned by the Landmark Trust. Nelson's Tower and the field it occupies is owned by the National Trust and is freely open, with access through a gate alongside what was Towerhill Farm/Tower Lodge. This approach, with a full view of the tower obtained on immediately passing through the gate, is much less satisfactory than the original picturesque route up the spiral drive.

Nelson's Tower/Paxton Tower is a Grade II* Registered Historic Park and Garden.

Sources:

Burke, J. B., 1854. *A Visitation of the Seats and Arms of the Noblemen and Gentlemen of Great Britain and Ireland,* (London: Hurst and Blackett). This publication includes Augustus Butler's lithograph of Nelson's Tower reproduced here.

Cadw: Welsh Historic Monuments, 2002. *Register of Landscapes, Parks and Gardens of Special Historic Interest in Wales. Part 1: Parks and Gardens* (Cardiff: Cadw).

Davies, D., 1998. 'Nelson's Tower in Image and Word', *Carmarthenshire Antiquary* 34, 44-53.

Lloyd, T., Orbach, J. and Scourfield, R., 2006. *The Buildings of Wales: Carmarthenshire and Ceredigion* (New Haven: Yale University Press).

Sale Plan of Middleton Hall Estate, 1824. In Ludlow, N. D.,1995. Middleton Hall Assessment, Dyfed Archaeological Trust, unpublished report.

Stained glass windows commissioned in honour of Lord Nelson and his victory at Trafalgar.
Removed from the Tower for safe keeping
(photograph: M Ings - courtesy Carmarthenshire Museum)

Neuadd Fawr

A Adams Rice

The former park still retains some of its original character,
walled gardens remain, but the formal gardens have gone,
as have most of the ornate buildings.

Neuadd Fawr Mansion (photograph: courtesy of Carmarthenshire Museum)

NEUADD FAWR, Cilycwm (SN752418)

Neuadd Fawr's vast ruin lies nestled under the eastern escarpment of Mynydd Mallaen, between two of three cascades of mountain water, the nearest of which has an old quarry within its cwm, below Craig Rhosan. The former park still retains some of its original character, walled gardens continue to exist, but the formal gardens are being lost as well as most of the ornate buildings.

The derelict remains of this impressive and once important mansion consist of a series of enlargements. The first was built in the late 1770s on the foundations of a fifthteenth-century property, and then enlarged after 1831 with neoclassical facades. The last enlargement occurred in 1889 when a substantial Victorian extension was added to the rear. These enlargements were funded by arrangements made by the Campbell-Davys' ancestors to purchase or inherit land in and around Carmarthenshire, especially in the upper Tywi valley. Despite a great lack of male lineage, surname dropping, the change of spelling and hyphenization, the Campbell-Davys family managed to remain at Neuadd Fawr until the 1940s. Then a lack of money reserves, ill health and the dwindling number of domestic and agricultural labourers led to the decline of this extravagantly built mansion and its accompanying estate.

The gardens fell to the same fate as the mansion. Originally it was the Campbell-Davys' new-found wealth in the mid to late nineteenth century that allowed such a grand house to be built in the beautiful and fertile landscape of the upper Tywi valley. Together with the rebuilt mansion were a planned parkland, ornamental garden buildings, tree plantings near the house, walled gardens for pleasure, leisure, and food production, and built water courses that brought needed supplies from the picturesque cascade behind the mansion. This cascade was fortuitously adjacent to a bed of rock that was quarried by house masons.

Throttled by a tree, the eastern façade in 2015 with remains of former parapets reused as a balustrade on the grass below (photograph: A Adams Rice)

149

The ruin of the mansion is approached by a private drive. At the park entrance stands a double wooden gateway hung between two stone pillars with an excellent rare spear and hinge design that is common in this area. An elm

Upper walled garden with newly planted fruit and nut trees in protective cages. View of Rhosan waterfall and quarry through northern gate (photograph: A Adams Rice)

avenue, destroyed by disease in the 1970s, once grew along the drive in this area leading to the main road. The ruined mansion is in private hands and is unsafe to enter.

Stock still graze in the 44 acres (18 hectares) of parkland, in which are mature trees – three magnificent wellingtonia, a row of nine elms and ancient oaks. The eastern façade of the mansion is now almost covered by a strangling copse that is spreading out of the central recess. This spread is creeping towards both end pilasters that frame the large low ground floor windows of the library and so-called Blue Room. The Billiard Room is centrally recessed on the ground floor and has a frontage of squared pillars beneath a narrow upper balcony with iron railings. It once had direct access, through full length windows, to the garden. At the turn of the nineteenth century, the parapets were tumbled from their heights as a safety precaution and were then reused as a feature in the garden below. All that remains of that parapet is a small mound of rubble stone lying on the northern edge of the grass frontage.

Here were once two beech hedges between which was a ha-ha-like ditch that was filled with rhododendron plantings, now removed. Below these hedges, breached by the remaining flight of wide steps, was a lower grassed area. Now only part of a single beech hedge remains. This lower formal area, that once featured a grass tennis court, is heavily planted with individual mature trees such as oak, Douglas fir, wild cherry, copper beech and Lawson cypress. There is a slope along the base of the grassed area going down to a length of wrought iron estate railings, which are divided by a hunting gate of the same design and material. This gate leads from the formal gardens into the parklands.

To the north of the mansion's Victorian extension is a grassy walled garden that once grew vegetables, soft fruit and cut flowers for the house. There was a central water supply from a sunken holding tank. On the extension wall is a roofless small bothy with slate-coloured tiled floor and pointed arched door and window. At the lower end of the walled garden is an original tŷ bach (privy). Remains of fruit training wire attachments and heating ironmongery from demolished hot-houses are still visible on the north wall. The east wall also has the remains of wooden soft fruit training supports and the access into the now derelict Victorian kitchen garden can be seen in the lower east corner.

On the other side of the narrow track outside the walled kitchen garden is another gate in a high wall built of pale yellow Ruabon bricks. Through this gate is a larger walled garden, reputed to measure a perfect square acre. In fact, the present owners have measured the area and found that it over an acre at 70 x 80 yards.

After the upper walled garden was built with three wide entrances to the west, south and north with cart wide paths, an orchard was planted within it. Mature walnut trees still exist in the upper area. When the present owners took over the estate, they ploughed up the walled area and seeded it with grass for grazing. The three entrances are now secured with modern steel farm gates. The watering point is still to be found in the lower half of this upper garden. Recently, new locally-sourced orchard stock of apple, pear, cherry, plum and damson has been planted. Sheep now graze between the protective fruit tree cages.

Through the centrally placed northern entrance gap is an arresting distant view of the Rhosan waterfall, at the base of which the main built water course to the mansion and pasture lands begins. This water course was skilfully engineered to fall 50 feet in every half mile along a line of rock face towards the Mansion. It is situated on the lower slopes of Mynydd Mallaen. An interesting exposed water junction point can be found in the pasture next to the west wall of the newly planted orchard. Here can be

Parklands with mature trees of Wellingtonia, lime and oak
(photograph: A Adams Rice)

seen glazed tiles, bricks and also glazed water pipes that still lead into the two walled gardens and beyond to the mansion. A section of this source has a slate-covered junction in the field behind the stable block, and forks off to the outside of a kennel area. Another water source is gathered in a 15 foot domed catch tank that is situated high amongst the slopes of mountain forestry growing directly behind the mansion.

Between the two walled gardens is a row of low buildings. They used to accommodate the hot-house boiler system and an apple store, next to which is a perforated aperture behind which cheeses were probably stored. At the top is the old potting shed. Around the corner are the kennels, with a small building next to them with a cooking fire place, which was used for preparing the dogs' feed.

Opposite the old kennel complex is the ruin of a handsome listed stable block built in the 1830s. This once delightful, now derelict building was built for housing the horses used for leisure activities. It still retains an early example of a ceiling using metal beams every 18 inches with strengthening concrete in between, creating a strong suspended floor to the hayloft above, where three lunette windows face out on to the rear lane. On the ground floor, remains can be found of the original partitioned stalls with artefacts for lodging and feeding the family horses. Oblong vents in the back wall of the stable block still let in fresh air. The exterior side walls are now overgrown with saplings.

Further down the northern rear lane, tucked up to the rear of the mansion and facing towards Home Farm, is the roofless shell of a desolate listed coach-house. Its glory days are over, for it once housed grand coaches and then the motoring transport for the Campbell-Davys family. The once ornate building is now flanked on each side of the missing double doors, by damaged arched windows and above these are delicate lunettes set on both sides of a once superb double ogee window. High in the central gable is a stone roundel that previously housed a carriage clock. The roof once supported a tower with a copper cupola. Nowadays the coach-house's dereliction is awesome.

The main southern façade of Neuadd Fawr mansion, with its neoclassical wrapping of stucco, is in a similar state of disrepair. The central heavy iron entrance porch that is supported by four fluted and decorated cast iron pillars has almost disappeared under swags of greenery. An ornamental double wrought-iron gate, hanging between two falling stone pillars flanked by two single gates of matching design, are a reminder of the elegance of the mansion and its gardens, for this set of gates used to link family, visitors and employees from the front door of the colossal mansion to the attractions of the coach-house and the stable.

Façade engulfed with greenery. In the foreground ornamental gates lead to the ruined coach-house and stable (photograph: A Adams Rice)

Nearby Home Farm was once the laundry and bake-house of the estate. It has an eastern-facing lawn edged with herbaceous flower and shrub borders. An aerial view of Home Farm shows clearly the outlines of a second tennis court centred on the lawn. This court was laid over a filled-in pond that reputedly, with the stream that fed it, used to dry up when a member of the Campbell-Davys family was dying.

A slow-moving black-cobbled rill runs through a corner of the farmhouse garden. This rill runs downhill through pasture from its source on Mynydd Mallean, to pass

Hunting gate leading from formal gardens to parklands
(photograph: A Adams Rice)

under the yard close to Home Farm and out into the cultivated garden, on through the Neuadd Fawr meadows until it reaches the mill north of Cilycwm village.

Across the lower yard of Home Farm stands a Victorian folly-fronted, high-stone barn with a castellated façade once topped by a cross. The cross fell during a storm in the 1990s and now rests against the yard wall.

Towards the road there is an early nineteenth century restored gothic lodge with an elegant incised milestone by its front wall border. The original drive to the mansion's main entrance porch and doors started here through the ornamental double gates. Along this approach drive are the remains of a stone bridge which has disappeared except for a small amount of stonework, but the culvert of the water course that leads away from the estate, which once passed under that bridge, can still be seen today.

Sources:

Notes and photographs taken during meetings with Aled Owen Edwards at Home Farm from July 2015 and onwards into 2016. Additional sources from Dai and Joan Edwards.

Ordnance Survey 1:2500 First Edition map.

Blaenau Tywi History Group, 2014. *Enwau yn y Tirwedd Blaenau Tywi/Names in the Landscape Blaenau Tywi*, (Llandysul: Blaenau Tywi History Group).

Davies, R., 2005. *Hope and Heartbreak*, (Cardiff: University of Wales Press).

Fenton, R., 1917. *Tours in Wales, 1804-1813* (Cambrian Archaeological Association).

Hill, L. G., 1947. *The Vale of Towy* (Hereford: Jakemans Limited).

Jones, F., 1987. *Historic Carmarthenshire Homes and their Families* (Carmarthen: Carmarthenshire Antiquarian Society).

Lloyd, T., 1986. *The Lost Houses of Wales* (London: Save Britain's Heritage).

Lloyd, T., Orbach, J. and Scourfield, R., 2006. *The Buildings of Wales: Carmarthenshire and Ceredigion* (New Haven: Yale University Press).

Walford Davies, D., Dafydd, S.M. and White, P., 2012. *Ancestral Houses: The Lost Mansions of Wales* (Llandysul: Gomer Press).

Folly façade of stone barn
(photograph: A Adams Rice)

Fallen cross that once topped the barn
façade (photograph: A Adams Rice)

Pantglas Hall

J Holland

The record in the Cadw Register of Historic Parks and Gardens reads: 'much of the Victorian gardens (including a lake), constructed to complement the Italianate mansion built about 1853, remains intact although the house has gone.'

Old photograph, Pantglas Hall (courtesy Carmarthenshire Museum)

PANTGLAS, Llanfynydd (SN548256)

The record in the Cadw Register of Historic Parks and Gardens reads: *'much of the Victorian gardens (including a lake), constructed to complement the Italianate mansion built about 1853, remains intact although the house has gone.'*

Today part of the site is a timeshare leisure facility and little remains of the once fine gardens, terraces and borders. The structures and framework of the garden and woodlands survive with mature specimen trees, the single tower of the mansion, a small ornamental bridge, the lake, the coach house and stable courtyard and the walled garden and the potting sheds.

Old postcard of Pantglas Hall and grounds (courtesy of P Davies)

Pantglas is situated 12km north-east of Carmarthen and 1.5km north-west of Llanfynydd. Francis Jones records John Jones, an attorney at law as the earliest known resident in the late seventeenth century. The property passed to his great grandson Richard. Richard married Alicia Gratiana Williams, who inherited the property when Richard died in 1799. A copy of her will can be found in the National Library of Wales in which she left the property to Nicholas Burnell, a descendent of the family and a captain in the East India trade. It was left on the condition that he took the surname Jones and *'shall reside in Pantglas Hall and Demesne as his principle country residence (and shall keep the same in repair)'*.

Nicholas Burnell inherited the estate in 1806, and sold it in 1822. At that time it included 50 properties. The mansion was T-shaped described in the sale particulars as: *'a commodious mansion, seated in a paddock of about 60 acres with sundry valuable farms, containing 708 acres of rich arable pasture and woodland, several other farms and tenements about 988 acres'*. It was sold on 20 June 1822 at auction in London.

The house at that time comprised a drawing room, dining room, library, gentleman's room or study, breakfast room, two staircases and butler's pantry, kitchen, bakehouse, servant's hall and appropriate domestic offices. Detached offices included a laundry, malting house, brewhouse and kiln and a small house adjoining for the gardener, a 6-stall stable and loft over and coach house. It describes the grounds: *'commanding most delightful views'* and a *'capital fish pond fully supplied with fish of all descriptions, a productive garden and a dog kennel.'*

The house was sold to a David Jones, a Llandovery banker, whose son David was responsible for the construction of the Italianate mansion and landscaped gardens. The original mansion may have been incorporated into the new building which was completed in 1854. The estate was left to his daughter who sold it in 1919, to a Mr Lewis, who sold it on shortly afterwards to the local authority to be used as an asylum.

The mansion continued as an asylum until 1965 when it was badly damaged by fire. It is recorded in the sale details of 1972 that the day-room, cloakroom, patient's dining room, occupational therapy room, six dormitories, and two store rooms were damaged by the fire. It was sold at auction to a developer, who demolished the mansion leaving only the tower and part of the portico standing.

Very little remains of the planting, terraces and borders that were created around the Italianate mansion in the 1850s. There were three entrances, with three lodges.

Photograph: courtesy of G Hudson

The main entrance to the south, entered through a set of imposing iron gates; it passed over the bridge branching to the house and coach house. This was disused after the estate became an asylum. The western entrance, beside the Keepers Lodge, follows three sides of the walled garden to the Home Farm and was a tradesman and working entrance. The drive on the north side was originally to the west of the lodge and had white painted wooden gates; it has since moved to the south-east side of the lodge, one branch runs to join the drive to the north of the walled garden and south to the stable block and house. This is now the main entrance to the grounds.

The walled garden is to the north of the mansion, enclosing an area of 1.5 acres. The walls are in good condition and are about 3m high, mainly of rubble stone, with brick showing where the stove flues would have been in the south wall. The remains of wall-trained fruit trees are in evidence on the south-facing north wall. On the internal south wall were the potting sheds, fruit room and lumber room with heated vinery and peach house on the external wall, all of which are shown on the 1906 Ordnance Survey 1:2500 map. The brick base of one survives, which may have been restored when the mansion was an asylum. Today the upper half of the walled garden is tarmacked with tennis courts and gymnasium, sauna and swimming pool complex while the lower half is grassed and contains a children's play area and crazy golf course.

Below the walled garden to the south is a rectangular area of grass which may have been tennis courts. To the south-west of the house were croquet lawns. Black and white photographs of the mansion show elaborate flower borders on terraces descending in front of the house. The house site is now surrounded by hoarding boards, and there is no sign remaining of the once elaborate borders. The conservatory on the south-west of the house has not survived.

All of the old house was demolished after a fire with the exception of the tower which stands in a perilous state (photograph: J Holland)

The house was on an east-facing slope, which drops down to the lake, created in the 1850s. The lake was oval in shape with a small circular island. It had a gravelled path around it with flower borders, ornamental shrubs and specimen trees. The borders and shrubs have gone, but some specimen trees survive including a rare *Cupressus torulosa* and weeping beeches, *Fagus sylvatica*. The lake was drained between the First and Second World Wars for safety, breaching the retaining wall, but was re-instated after 1972. There was originally another pond. Today the lake has been extended to incorporate the bridge, with water on both sides.

The ornamental bridge, in the classical style, lies to the south of the stable block. It has a single span of coursed and squared stone blocks, a rounded arch and is flanked by pilasters. The parapet is balustraded.

To the north of the bridge is the stable block and coach house. This forms a rectangular block around a court yard, with the north and south ranges being two-storeyed while the east and west are single storeyed. The entrances to each range are through the archway on the southern side, with entrances from the inside of the courtyard. A stone above the arch gives the date 1851. A later addition on the north side gives another entrance to the second floor. Originally stabling and coach house, they became laundries, club premises with an entertainment hall, oak strip floors, dining room on the ground floor, with two staff bedrooms, and three dormitories and bedrooms above, for the asylum. They have since been converted into a reception entrance, a café and restaurant and laundries for the leisure facility.

The north drive is lined with laurel and a border on the eastern side. The laurels on the west are extremely tall, while those on the other side of the drive have been cut to form a low hedge.

The woodlands that cover the southern side of the estate survive but are now interspersed with wooden chalets. The chalets are quite discreet, but the grounds have a neglected feel, and brambles are competing with the planting around the lake. There are still mature plantings of exotics. The fastigiate yews that once bordered the croquet lawn are now towering giants.

Willaim Spurrell in 1879 described Pantglas: *'great taste has been exercised in decorating the house and laying out the ground.'* In 1904 The Carmarthen Weekly Reporter printed *'Pantglas is*

The entrance to the stable block at Pantglas is now used as a reception area for countryside holidays
(photograph courtesy J Holland)

ensconced amid some of the best woodland scenery in the far famed Vale of Towy, and it is of course among the best sporting estates for gun, rod and dogs."

Today it still enjoys glorious views, but essentially the once fine and abundant gardens are gone. It is under threat from development. Plans to build a large number of additional chalets to form a holiday village have been rejected, but it is possible the number will be reduced and a new application may be granted in the future.

Pantglas is a Grade II Registered Historic Park and Garden.

Sources:

British Newspaper Archive.

Cadw: Welsh Historic Monuments, 2002. *Register of Landscapes, Parks and Gardens of Special Historic Interest in Wales. Part 1: Parks and Gardens* (Cardiff: Cadw).

Jones, F., 1987. *Historic Carmarthenshire Homes and their Families* (Carmarthen: Carmarthenshire Antiquarian Society).

Lloyd, T., 1986. *The Lost Houses of Wales* (London: Save Britain's Heritage).

National Library of Wales, Pantglas Sale Particulars, 1822 and 1972.

Ordnance Survey 1:2500 First and Second Edition maps.

Spurrell, W., 1879. *Carmarthen and its Neighbourhood* (Carmarthen: Spurrell).

Bridge at Pantglas (photograph: J Holland)

Parc Howard

E Davies

The park entered public ownership, and gained its present name, due to a philanthropic gesture by Sir Stafford Howard in 1911 in a locally well-known tale given in brief below. Howard bought the property to make a gift of it to the people of Llanelli to celebrate his then recent marriage to Lady Howard Stepney.

Old postcard (courtesy P Davies)

PARC HOWARD, Llanelli (SN507011)

The mansion and gardens of Parc Howard as they appear today form a publicly owned park and are broadly split into four main areas as follows:

The eastern end is a large open grassed space encircled by a tree lined path

The central area to the south and south west of the mansion consists of formal gardens, with small lawns with wide flower beds surrounding them and feature planting in the centre; the duck pond, sunken remembrance garden and bandstand are also in this area. The whole is screened from the road to the south and the nearby housing to the south and west by closely planted mature trees of mostly sycamore and beech. Occasional planting of more exotic trees in the open spaces between break up the lawn spaces to the west of the mansion.

The north-western end of the park includes the playground, tennis courts, bowling green and clubhouse.

The northern end of the park lies over the lip of the ridge where the land drops away steeply and includes an outdoor paddling pool, Gorsedd circle, a play area for older children and more open grassland.

Most of the land occupies a southerly aspect with the northern end dropping steeply into a river valley on the side. The park entered public ownership, and gained its present name, due to a philanthropic gesture by Sir Stafford Howard in 1911 in a locally well-known tale given in brief below. Howard bought the property to make a gift of it to the people of Llanelli to celebrate his then recent marriage to Lady Howard Stepney, on the proviso that the grounds be transformed into a public park by their first anniversary by the town council. Over the years numerous alterations and additions have been made but prior to

Bandstand in the park, c.1900 old postcard (courtesy: P Davies)

the events of 1911-12 the gardens and mansion had undergone significant changes during the preceding century including a significant rebuild of the house.

The property was previously known as Bryn-y-Caerau and would not appear to be linked with any ancient seat or titles from documentary searches. The property and much of the surrounding land does not appear on the tithe map of Llanelli parish (1842) which strongly suggests it was not an established mansion and gardens by that time.

Old postcard (courtesy: P Davies)

The first known owner was a Mr R T Howell; a successful local business man rather than a member of the local aristocracy, which could be taken to further support a mid-nineteenth century date for its foundation.

The property and gardens were first depicted on the First Edition Ordnance Survey 1:2500 map of 1878. Initially the property only consisted of a narrow strip of land, running back from the road front on the A476 to the top of the ridge on which it sits, with a lodge

located to the west of the road entrance. The building occupied the very centre of the strip with gardens to the left and right of the mansion (the original building faced south-west not south-east as today). The lower garden is set out very formally with a driveway running along the southwest boundary line from the road to the entrance of the mansion. The remainder of the garden was taken up with a U-shaped footpath enclosing a small lawn and fountain feature, and other linking paths. The map markings indicate that the majority of the garden planting consisted of mixed tree and shrub planting, which may have been done to create a more private setting in an otherwise open field. Two other features in the lower garden as noted by the Ordnance Survey were a sundial and a gun stand although no information relating to either is known. The upper gardens are shown as being set out on a rectangular pattern, with orderly tree planting. It is highly likely that the small buildings in this area included the working buildings such as stable blocks, as was the case later in its history. The orderly nature of the planting may suggest that this was an orchard or nuttery, given its location.

Upon Mr R T Howell's death the property passed to a distant relative, Mr James Buckley Wilson, an architect, who personally designed and oversaw the additions and alterations that created the Italianate mansion of today. The Second Edition OS map of 1905 shows that some additions and changes were made to the garden at this time, including that the driveway was pushed into a wider loop to the south-west while most of the footpaths and garden features of the earlier garden were removed and a fish pond incorporated. The grounds are shown to have spread outwards to the south-east and south-west from the original narrow strip of the First Edition OS map, with the boundaries being less rigid and more curved. The prominence of mixed trees and shrubs in the planting regime would appear to have continued and even spread in places, but the impression given is that the planting may have been sparser.

The sale of Bryn-y-Caerau to Sir Stafford Howard took place in 1911 as previously stated. His proviso for works to be undertaken to convert the gardens for public use resulted in the creation of a sunken garden in the south, and the erection of a bandstand and a seating area with a dance floor known as the *'amphitheatre'* to the west of the mansion itself.

Photograph: E Davies

Old postcard (courtesy P Davies)

Further additions were made over the next 100 years including more paths, a Gorsedd stone-circle that was erected for the 1962 Eisteddfod, tennis courts, a bowling green and a children's' playground, while others were lost or altered like the bandstand and amphitheatre.

Given that the grounds were greatly celebrated prior to the gardens passing into public possession, their heyday could be considered as being between their opening in 1911 and the present, due to their expansion and development during this period and the increased variety of planting and garden areas provided.

Parc Howard is a Grade II Registered Historic Park and Garden.

Sources:

Cadw: Welsh Historic Monuments, 2002. *Register of Landscapes, Parks and Gardens of Special Historic Interest in Wales. Part 1: Parks and Gardens* (Cardiff: Cadw).

Ordnance Survey First and Second Edition 1:2500 maps, 1878 and 1905.

Pembrey Country Park

M Ings

One of Wales's top visitor attractions offering many
recreational activities including cycling, horse-riding,
crazy golf and a miniature steam railway.

The skeleton of a wreck on Pembrey Sands (photograph: M Ings)

Pembrey Country Park (SN405004)

The name Pembrey derives from an anglicisation of the Welsh, Pen-bre. 'Pen' meaning head or top, and 'bre' being a headland.

The landscaped forestry and parkland that border the eight mile expanse of Cefn Sidan beach is now advertised as one of Wales's top visitor attractions offering many recreational activities including cycling, horse-riding, crazy golf and a miniature steam railway.

The park is located on a dynamic dune system, the central part of the Pembrey Burrows that form one of a number of dune systems fringing the eastern part of Carmarthen Bay. The dunes create a barrier to the coast, impeding drainage of the land behind and creating extensive tidal flats and marshes. Attempts to stabilize the sand and prevent dune migration first entailed using brushwood fencing and marram. In 1928 The Forestry Commission acquired the land that was to become Pembrey Forest and mostly planted Corsican pine, together with some Sitka pine, Norway spruce and sea buckthorn.

Such diverse habitat is home to a wide variety of flora and fauna. A local nature reserve has been established at Pembrey Saltmarsh which, together with the dunes, is designated a SSSI (a Site of Special Scientific Interest). Nature trails have been created throughout the Park. Many species of plants are to be found, including dune pansies, rock sea lavender and green-winged orchids. Insects include many butterfly species, including the small blue, green hairstreak and marbled white, and rare moths such as the grass eggar moth and the burnished brass moth. Bird hides have been set up in the conservation area, overlooking two shallow pools and otters have recently been spotted.

It may come as a surprise to hear that such a tranquil and picturesque spot has a rather explosive past. Its relative remoteness made it attractive for the manufacture of dynamite, first for mining and industrial purposes in the late nineteenth century and then, during the two World Wars, to make munitions. During the First World War there were two factories

Pill boxes once part of The Stop line can still be found across the park (photograph: M Ings)

covering a huge area, 760 acres, and employing over 6000 people, mostly women, from Llanelli, Carmarthen and Swansea. Some of the earthworks, built as blast banks around the buildings where explosives were made, still survive today. These buildings were almost completely demolished in 1938 when construction started on the Royal Ordnance Factory which became the largest supplier of TNT during the Second World War, employing 3000 men and women.

Pine plantations (photograph: M Ings)

The Second World War has also a number of installations designed to protect the open expanse of Cefn Sidan beach and the nearby airfield. These included anti-landing obstacles and pill-boxes which formed part of a strategic Command Stop Line that extended from Carmarthen Bay to New Quay on Ceredigion Bay. Pembrey was bombed on the 10 July 1940 and 10 workers were killed – the first day of the Battle of Britain.

During the 1960s there was an attempt to establish a munitions testing range at the site but a successful 'Save Our Sands' campaign mounted by locals led to the establishment of Pembrey Country Park instead, opening on 1 August 1980.

Skeletal timbers embedded in the shoreline sands are further testament to a violent past. Carmarthen Bay is infamously treacherous for shipping, with broad intertidal ranges and an abundance of sandbanks, and many ships have foundered here. Not that it was always natural obstacles at the heart of disaster. There are stories told of the 'Gwyr y Bwelli Bach', or 'People of the little hatchets', Pembrey locals who would attract ships to their doom with misleading signal beacons in order to loot valuables from passengers and crew. One of Carmarthen Bay's most notorious shipwrecks occurred in 1828, when *La Jeune Emma*, a French brig bound from the West Indies with a cargo of rum, sugar and coffee, ran aground on the Cefn Sidan sands with a loss of thirteen lives. Among those to perish was Adeline Coquelin, the 12-year old niece of Napoleon Bonaparte's consort, Josephine. She is buried at St. Illtyds Church, Pembrey. A contemporary account (Cambrian Quarterly) tells of how the stricken crew were robbed and ill-treated by looters, who had done their worst before the Royal Carmarthen Militia arrived to protect the wreck.

Thankfully it is not easy to imagine such horrors when enjoying the peaceful splendour of Cefn Sidan today. It is a vast expanse, especially when the tide is out and the sea and sky merge in a shimmering haze of silver punctuated by the sinuous, translucence of the

Gower coastline. Often promoted as one of the finest beaches in Britain, if not Europe, Cefn Sidan has been awarded Blue Flag status in recognition of its high environmental and quality standards. The Bay now plays host to a variety of activities, including swimming, sand-yachting and parasailing.

The park is open daily from dawn to dusk. Facilities include a caravan and camping site, a visitor centre, children's playgrounds and a café.

Sources

Bennet T., 1992, *Shipwrecks around Wales, Volume 1.*

Davidson A. (ed.), 2002, CBA Research Report 131, *The coastal archaeology of Wales.*

Davies J. et al, 2008, *The Encyclopaedia of Wales.*

James, H. (ed.), 1991, *Sir Gar, Studies in Carmarthenshire History.*

Nicholson J.A., *1978, Pembrey St. Illtyd's Church with Llandyry.*

Pye K. & Blott S., 2014, NRW Evidence Report no.42, *Pembrey Burrows – a geomorphological appraisal and options for dune rejuvenation.*

Pyper A., forthcoming, Pembrey Country Park leaflet.

The Lake, Pembrey Country Park (photograph: M Ings)

Stradey Castle

J Holland

A fine terraced garden is associated with the mid-nineteenth century mansion. Within the park are some interesting water features, a good range of trees, including some early introductions, and a woodland walk. A fine walled garden and nursery area are associated with the seventeenth-century house.

Old postcard (courtesy P Davies)

STRADEY CASTLE, Llanelli (SN491153)

Stradey Castle is a Grade II* Listed building and the park and gardens are listed Grade II. Cadw's *Register of Landscapes Parks and Gardens of Special Historical Interest in Wales* gives the reasons for grading: '*There is a fine terraced garden associated with the mid-nineteenth century mansion. Within the park are some interesting water features, a good range of trees, including some early introductions, and a woodland walk. A fine walled garden and nursery area are associated with the seventeenth-century house, whose site was turned into a garden in the mid nineteenth century*'.

Stradey became an estate when the land was purchased by the Vaughans of Derwydd in the early seventeenth century. John Mansel married Mary, the daughter of Sir Henry Vaughan, and settled at Stradey. It remained the property of the Vaughans until 1673 when 510 acres were sold to John Mansel's grandson. It remained in the Mansel family until Mary Anne Mansel inherited the estate from her brother and, having no children of her own, she left it to Thomas Lewis of Llandeilo in 1808. Thomas Lewis was the family lawyer and friend, who had secured the release from debtors' prison of Sir Edward Vaughan Mansel. Sir Edward had been imprisoned in Carmarthen Gaol, and later in the Fleet Prison in London, due to financial difficulties. The family added the surname Mansel to that of Lewis and the estate has remained in the family to this day.

The original house faced south-east and was an L-shaped building on the banks of the Afon Dulais; overlooking the park to the north, it was separated from the park by a ha-ha. It had outbuildings to the north and gardens and grounds on its southern and eastern side. Across the river was the orchard field and woodland. It was probably built by John Mansel who died in 1675. It sat on level ground just to the north of the present Pembrey to Llanelli road.

A watercolour sketch painted by Laetitia Mansel Lewis, which now hangs in Stradey Castle, shows a three-storeyed house with a pillared portico entrance. The picture shows a house with an open aspect with cows grazing in the foreground and a wooded hillside behind. Each storey has a range of nine windows. Between 1820 and 1830 the house was enlarged and by 1829 there were thirty three rooms. The walled garden and nursery are associated with this house.

In 1844 Mr David Mansel Lewis commissioned the architect Edward Haycock of Shrewsbury to design and build a new house on the higher ground, 300m to the north. This was completed in 1855. The earlier house was demolished, but the garden around the house remained, together with the ha-ha.

The new mansion, Stradey Castle, is a large neo-Tudor country house facing south, with the main entrance on the north side. It has extensive views over the parkland to the south and to the sea beyond. It was added to in the 1870s. Charles William Mansel Lewis was a talented painter and needed a studio, with a skylight. To achieve this, the mansion was extended with a billiard room on the ground floor and studio above, with a flat roof to allow for a skylight. To maintain the balance of the house a tower was added to the end of the house in 1874. The battlemented tower is 40 feet high and the top of the tower is reached by an external flight of stairs which rise from the adjoining flat roof. The terraces to the south and east of the house were added at that time.

The First Edition Ordnance Survey map shows a number of drives traversing the estate. Originally there were six lodges of which three survive, two to the north off the Trimsaran Road and one to the south on the Pembrey to Llanelli Road. The main entrance is off the Trimsarran road and runs to the south-west, curving around the north of the mansion and down towards the south. It joins the drive from the south, crosses the Afon Dulais over two single span bridges; the orchard field is passed on the right and the entrance to the original house on the left. The drive follows the walls of the walled garden, past the cottages, the mill, sawmill and granary, to join the Pembrey to Llanelli Road at the bottom.

The parkland and gardens are made up of a number of elements: a flat area of open parkland below and to the south of the mansion; the walled garden and nursery; the terraces to the south and east; the woodland to the north and west of the house, and the old garden of the earlier house. Coleg Sir Gâr now occupies part of the grounds between the park and the main road. The estate once included the rugby ground now occupied by the Scarlets. Originally loaned to the town for recreation - rugby, football and cricket, the relationship was formalised in1902 with a lease to the Rugby and Football Club.

Opposite the front door and to the north of the house is a small dipping well, with a scalloped bowl. It has a trickle of water into the bowl, through the mouth of a carved lion's head, and dates from around 1850. Beside the well are steps leading to woodland walks above the house.

The main terrace in front of the house, overlooking the park (photograph: J Holland)

Stradey Castle undergoing repairs 2015
(photograph: J Holland)

To the east and south of the house is a broad terrace, with a rectangle of box hedges either side of a stone lily pond. There are borders around the house, and a magnolia on the end of the building. The terrace has a low wall surrounding it, and separating it from the parkland below.

From the terrace across the open parkland to the south, you can see the Wilderness Garden. This was the site of the gardens around the original house. It was maintained until the early 1900s but was neglected between the Wars, and became overgrown. The woodland garden has been restored with the help of Mr Leslie Baker, the son of one of the estate workers, who took up the challenge on his retirement. The Wilderness Garden has become a small arboretum with camellias and rhododendrons around the lake. The eighteenth century fountain has been restored.

The walled garden is triangular and was part of the grounds of the earlier house. The walls are in good condition, although the service buildings are in ruins. The First Edition Ordnance Survey map shows an extensive range of glasshouses against the stable and cottage wall, to the north wall of the walled garden. On the opposite side of the drive is a nineteenth-century granary, with arched openings, and the ruins of the flour mill, and saw mill. Brunel is said to have been involved in the design of the water running through the site to power the mills and water features. The walled garden is now leased to a market gardener. The First Edition Ordnance Survey map gives the description Spring Nursery to the west of the southern lodge where the drive emerges onto the main road. There has been a nursery associated with this site for at least two hundred years.

To the west of the house and to the south-west is woodland, with woodland walks. Immediately adjacent to the house is a group of conifers and deciduous trees which include a Scots pine. There were several small lakes or ponds, including a smaller skating pond. The river Dulais runs along the boundary of the Wilderness garden. The ponds have largely disappeared but the area can be identified by wetter ground.

The current owners Patrick and Claire Mansel Lewis open the house and grounds by arrangement for heritage tours, wedding parties and photo-shoots.

Stradey Castle is a Grade II Registered Historic Park and Garden.

Sources:
Cadw: Welsh Historic Monuments, 2002. *Register of Landscapes, Parks and Gardens of Special Historic Interest in Wales. Part 1: Parks and Gardens* (Cardiff: Cadw).

Guided tour by Patrick and Claire Mansel Lewis.

Jones, F., 1987. *Historic Carmarthenshire Homes and their Families* (Carmarthen: Carmarthenshire Antiquarian Society).

Paintings in Stradey Castle.

www.stradeycastle.com

The Rockery - Wilderness Garden (postcard: courtesy P Davies)

174

Taliaris

K Arblaster

The grounds have had a chequered existence: the walled gardens were used for schooling horses in the 1970s, when part of the wall was dismantled for access, and in the 1990s they were used as an area for quiet retreat by the Sati Society. Since then the house has had several different owners but as yet no-one has tried to recreate the historic garden layout.

Old postcard (courtesy P Davies)

TALIARIS, Llandeilofawr Rural (SN639279)

The oldest part of Taliaris mansion is believed to date from at least 1630. The earliest known owners were the Gwynne family. Judicious marriages throughout the following century kept the estate in reasonable heart. In 1721 David Gwynne died childless and left the property to his great nephew, Richard Jones of Tregib, on condition that he took his name. Shortly after his marriage to Ann Rudd in 1722 Richard had Taliaris mansion re-fronted in Bath stone. From the south and east the house seems to be a grand three storey mansion. The other two sides, though, were untouched and remain a jumble of different styles and roof lines.

By 1785 the estate was sold to Lord Robert Seymour. He was a keen agricultural improver and encouraged the tenants on the 3,000 acre estate to use new methods of husbandry. Following his death, the estate was sold once again in 1833 to Robert Peel, an industrialist from Lancashire who also had interests in Radnorshire. His descendants finally ended their association with the estate when Taliaris house and the few acres surrounding it were sold in 1967. Since then the grounds have had a chequered existence: the walled gardens were used for schooling horses in the 1970s, when part of the wall was dismantled for access, and in the 1990s they were used as an area for quiet retreat by the Sati Society (a religious group). Since then the house has had several different owners but as yet no-one has tried to recreate the historic garden layout.

The walled garden stands to the south-east of the house. It covers about 1.75 acres and the walls are a maximum height of 3m. It is roughly triangular, with a wall from east to west dividing the space and creating a second triangle. The remains of stone-built tool sheds and the gardeners' bothy adjoin this wall; the north wall of the upper garden is brick-faced on the inside and has remnants of a brick-built base of a glass-house – there are signs of a heating flue on the far side.

Early maps show irregular paths through the walled gardens but it is hard to make out anything more of the layout. Edward Knight visited Taliaris in 1760 and referred to it as a *'small garden in the old taste'*. He described its situation as *'among a large plantation of Firs'* and Richard Fenton, who visited 50 years later, wrote of it as *'surrounded on all sides by rich woods'*. Fenton probably approached the house along the carriage drive from the west, marked on the lane by a small lodge house. Today a public footpath starts off along this old drive way but then carries on towards Maerdy Wood while the drive veers north east towards the house. This first, wooded section contains a mixture of native and exotic species. The footpath passes through the parkland to the south of the house, which enjoys magnificent views across the Tywi valley to the Brecon Beacons.

To the north of the house, across the lane, is the woodland called The Warren on the OS map. The kidney-shaped lake called Llyn Taliaris and the remains of a boathouse are in these woods.

Taliaris Lake in the 1950s (courtesy Carmarthenshire Museum)

The lake was possibly formed from the *'four Fish Ponds'* referred to in sale particulars of 1785; it was certainly a single expanse by 1840. It is still possible to see some retaining walls around the lake, with an arrangement of channels and pipes. Back across the lane, where two minor roads meet, are the remains of a header pond that once powered a saw mill. The saw pit can also be found among the undergrowth. This mill is believed to be the only shaft -turbine water powered saw mill recorded in Wales; Robert Peel apparently spent years researching the system before having it installed in the 1880s.

It is believed that the layout of parkland gardens at Taliaris has been little changed for two hundred years. Although the site is not open to the public, it is possible to appreciate the setting and the views from the surrounding lanes and public footpaths.

Taliaris is a Grade II Registered Historic Park and Garden.

Sources:

Cadw: Welsh Historic Monuments, 2002. *Register of Landscapes, Parks and Gardens of Special Historic Interest in Wales. Part 1: Parks and Gardens* (Cardiff: Cadw).

www.Coflein.gov.uk

Tregib House

H Whitear

The former site of Tregib Mansion lies in the grounds of Tregib Comprehensive School. The house and land was bought by the County Council in 1960s as a site for the school, but the house was sadly demolished in the late 1970s, and the associated gardens became school playing fields.

Tregib House (courtesy Carmarthenshire Museum)

TREGIB, Dyffryn Cennen formerly Llandeilofawr parish (SN633213)

The former site of Tregib Mansion lies in the grounds of Tregib Comprehensive School. The house and land was bought by the County Council in 1964 as a site for the school, but the house was sadly demolished in the late 1970s, and the associated gardens became school playing fields. In 1996, the National Eisteddfod was held in Llandeilo, and the Gorsedd stones remain on the site of the mansion where they were erected for the event.

Tregib House and estate belonged to the Jones and Jones-Gwynne family, local gentry of some social standing. The earliest owner of Tregib recorded by Francis Jones was John ap Harry who died in 1555, followed by Morgan John who held office as Justice of the Peace (1581) and later High Sheriff (1602). His descendants (three of whom were High Sheriffs in 1647, 1676 and 1705) took the name Jones. In 1721 the family inherited the Taliaris estate from an uncle, David Gwynne, who had no children of his own. The estate passed via his sister (Mrs Sibyl Jones of Tregib) to her grandson Richard Jones on the condition that he took the surname Gwynne. The family adopted the name Jones-Gwynne, and in 1722 acquired more property through marriage. Despite this good fortune, the estate had been mortgaged so heavily by the late eighteenth century that a large part of it including Taliaris had to be sold in 1787. However, Tregib remained in the hands of the Jones-Gwynne family until its sale to the local authority in the mid twentieth century.

Late nineteenth-century photographs record Tregib house's final *'thoroughly Victorian'* incarnation (according to Frances Jones). The documented 1888-89 remodelling by David Jenkins of Llandeilo concealed a core of earlier fabric, much of which appears to have been of considerable antiquity. The house was described as having features of all ages from the fourteenth century onwards. Recording carried out by RCAHMW prior to demolition noted many medieval features inside the house. An unverified historical reference to a Gwilym ap Philip of Tre-Gib, Llandeilo Fawr at about 1330 seems to support the idea that Tregib house was in existence on or near this site by the early fourteenth century.

The presence of gardens surrounding the house during the late nineteenth century is attested by historic mapping and photographs of the time. First and Second Edition Ordnance Survey maps show that during the late nineteenth and early twentieth centuries the house was approached from the north-west, with the approach flanked by belts of deciduous and conifer trees. Numerous specimen trees survive today framing the somewhat less lovely school buildings, and the former approach (carriage driveway/road) is still visible on the ground (although very overgrown in places) as a hollow-way between two substantial parallel stone walls.

Surviving contemporary black and white images taken after the 1888-89 remodelling all depict the northwest façade of the house, with its formal multi-layered terraces decorated with ornamental trees and shrubs, and several broad flights of stone steps, (one aligned with what appears to be the front door at the time). This suggests that this façade had

An old postcard of Tregib House and setting (courtesy P Davies)

become important, and that some of the planting and terraces (still visible as earthworks and surviving masonry steps) might be contemporary with this remodelling.

A large rectangular pond is marked to the southwest of the house on the First Edition OS map of 1891, and on the Second Edition is labelled *'fish pond'*. It is also visible on aerial photographs, and apparently survived until the house was demolished by the council, when local people recall that it was infilled with much of the fabric of the house. Its location is still visible on the ground as a rectangular area which has remained clear of trees and shrubs. The pond's shape and formality might suggest a Victorian date. However, it is also marked on the parish Tithe map of 1841. Its location to the south-west of the house is slightly incongruous with the formal terraces and remodelled north-west frontage, but Tregib's parkland also lies mostly to the south-west of the house. A photograph of c.1871 which pre-dates the late Victorian remodelling, shows the south-west façade of the house, with the pond (full of lilies) providing a very attractive foreground viewed from parkland to the south-west. The rectangular shape of the pond is not reminiscent of the naturalised landscapes typical of the pre-Victorian era either, and so the pond could represent a survival from a much earlier phase in the house's history.

The course of the Afon Cib runs to the north of the house, but is diverted just south of Ty Cefn Tregib (former outbuildings and stables for Tregib House) into a channel which probably supplied the pond with water. A drain on the northwest side of the pond is still visible in woodland to the south of the school, alongside the former driveway. The channel supplying the pond seems to dictate the southern boundary of the large kitchen garden southeast of the house, supporting the idea that the pond pre-dated the larger walled enclosure. This shape of the kitchen garden is preserved today in the line of field boundaries, but the enclosing garden walls, and all associated garden buildings and glass houses were probably destroyed at the time the house was demolished.

Many of these historic garden elements survived long enough to be recorded on colour aerial photographs of the late 1960s. These photographs show a high stone wall enclosing a large area of garden to the southeast of the house, with an extra stone wall of similar height running externally along the north-east side, providing a slip garden. There is a row of probable out-buildings of one and a half stories with small dormer windows, backing onto the northeast wall close to the house. This section of the garden wall is really interesting as it is thick and is crenelated (perhaps another vestigial early garden feature - medieval?). It appears to have formed part of a smaller square walled courtyard garden immediately adjacent to the house. Further south-east, the south-west façade of the north-east inner wall is whitewashed, and faces into the larger (probably Victorian) walled garden area. Here, the footings of a building can be seen, next to a lean-to boiler house (on the north elevation of the inner wall of the slip garden). The presence of the boiler house suggests these were footings for a heated peach or pineapple house, again probably of Victorian date.

It seems that the large Victorian kitchen garden remained useful, and mostly functional, well into the twentieth century. In 1947 the house became a Catholic school, St. Mary's College, Tregib, which provided places for 50 boarders. The aerial photographs show a chapel building which was constructed against the north-east side of the inner north-east garden wall. The religious community were keen gardeners and sold their surplus vegetables in Llandeilo and Ffairfach. In 1958 the Catholic school moved to Cheltenham.

The antiquity of the building elements noted within the house prior to demolition, and features described above suggest a much earlier date for the origins of the formal gardens at Tregib, perhaps medieval. The house was remodelled on numerous occasions, but retained earlier elements, and this seems likely to have extended to the gardens as well. Multi-period formal garden features might be expected to survive as buried remains.

Sources:

Archaeologia Cambrensis, 1968. *Taliaris.*

Carmarthenshire Record Office, Cawdor/Vaughan mss, Plan of Golden Grove 1794.

Cambria Archaeology, An Assessment of Historic Parks and Gardens in the Tywi Valley, unpublished report.

Aerial photographs - Tregib House and Gardens - 'Catholic Llandeilo. Part 3': Google Earth; vertical aerial photograph 2143 106G/U.K.1625. 7th July 1946; two colour photographs, possibly late 1960s, courtesy of current owner of Ty Cefn Tregib.

Dyfed Cultural Services Department & the National Library of Wales, 1991. *Llandeilo, Llandovery and the Upper Tywi Valley in old photographs* (Stroud: Alan Sutton).

Jones, F., 1987. *Historic Carmarthenshire Homes and their Families* (Carmarthen: Carmarthenshire Antiquarian Society).

Llandeilo Fawr Parish Tithe Map, 1841.

Lloyd, T., 1986. *The Lost Houses of Wales* (London: Save Britain's Heritage).

Ordnance Survey 1:2500 First and Second Edition maps ,1891 and 1907.

RCAHMW, pictures and records in the National Monument Record, Aberystwyth.

Smith, P., 1988. *Houses of the Welsh Countryside* (London: HMSO).

Whittle, E., 1992. *The Historic Gardens of Wales* (Cadw). (London: HMSO). www.llandeilo.org Llandeilo Town website.

www.ourfamilyhistory.org : Our Family History website (reference to Gwilym ap Philip Abt 1330 of Tre-Gib, Llandeilo Fawr).

An old postcard c 1911, Tregib Mansion (courtesy P Davies)